Centers of Pedagogy

Agenda for Education in a Democracy
Timothy J. McMannon, Series Editor

Centers of Pedagogy

New Structures for Educational Renewal

Robert S. Patterson
Nicholas M. Michelli
Arturo Pacheco

Agenda for Education in a Democracy

Volume 2

Jossey-Bass Publishers
San Francisco

1999

Jossey-Bass books and products are available through most bookstores. To contact Jossey-Bass directly, call (888) 378–2537, fax to (800) 605–2665, or visit our website at www.josseybass.com.

Substantial discounts on bulk quantities of Jossey-Bass books are available to corporations, professional associations, and other organizations. For details and discount information, contact the special sales department at Jossey-Bass.

 Manufactured in the United States of America on Lyons Falls Turin Book. This paper is acid-free and 100 percent totally chlorine-free.

Library of Congress Cataloging-in-Publication Data

Patterson, Robert S.
  Centers of pedagogy : new structures for educational renewal / Robert S. Patterson, Nicholas M. Michelli, Arturo Pacheco.—1st ed.
    p. cm.—(Agenda for education in a democracy series; v. 2)
  Includes bibliographical references and index.
  ISBN 0-7879-4561-7
  1. Teachers—Training of—United States.   2. College-school cooperation—United States.   3. Teachers colleges—United States.
I. Michelli, Nicholas M., 1942–   II. Pacheco, Arturo, 1941–   III. Title.
IV. Series.
  LB1715.P29   1999
  370'.71—dc21   98-51244

PB Printing   10 9 8 7 6 5 4 3 2 1   FIRST EDITION

Contents

Series Foreword

In 1894, a young Theodore Roosevelt proclaimed, "There are two gospels which should be preached to every reformer. The first is the gospel of morality; the second is the gospel of efficiency."[1] The interplay of efficiency and morality in human institutions, particularly in the educational institutions we call schools, continues to intrigue.[2] On the surface, both morality and efficiency are good; *morality* denotes fairness, virtue, and good conduct, among other things, and *efficiency* bespeaks a high level of achievement or production with a minimal expenditure of effort, money, or time. Ideally, our schools, our governments, our places of employment, even our families would be both moral and efficient in their own ways.

Difficulties arise, however, when we attempt to move beyond generalizations to specifics. What is morality? Who decides? Philosophers far wiser than I have spent lifetimes trying to convince themselves and others that there are or there are not definitive answers to those brief but complex questions. How can efficiency be judged? What are the criteria? Again the questions point to no single, certain answers. Moreover, inefficiencies have frequently been imposed on human institutions in the name of efficiency, and immoralities promulgated in the name of morality. When we advance to another level of specificity and consider morality and efficiency in the schools, the questions not only retain their complexity but also become very personal and deadly serious: Should my child's school teach morality? What exactly would that mean? How efficient is the schooling my child is experiencing? Do my child's grades reflect actual learning? These and similar questions shape debates and decisions about our nation's schools.

Neil Postman argues that we come to understand our lives and ascribe meaning to our actions by placing them in the context of a narrative: "a story . . . that tells of origins and envisions a future, a story that constructs ideals, prescribes rules of conduct, provides a source of authority, and, above all, gives a sense of continuity and purpose."[3] If Postman is right—and I think he is—then our chosen narratives help both to determine and to reveal what we are willing to work for, to live for, perhaps even to die for.

Rarely, if ever, are people called on to give their lives in defense of the institution of the school or the process of education. Some heroic teachers have, of course, given their lives in defense of their students. Clearly, their narratives embraced selflessness and sacrifice. But for most educators, selflessness and sacrifice mean no more than forgoing other more lucrative and respected professions, giving up evenings and weekends to grade papers, or serving on interminable committees. Even these sacrifices represent hardships, however, and they raise questions about educators' narratives. What are teachers willing to work for, to give their lives *to?*

Educators in the sixteen settings of the National Network for Educational Renewal (NNER)—be they school faculty, teacher educators, or arts and sciences professors—have chosen to embrace a morally based narrative for education and schooling. They see schools as places where democracy is learned and practiced, where schooling is far more than job training, where education is a seamless process of self-improvement. To them, teaching must be guided by a four-part mission: enculturating the young in a social and political democracy, providing access to knowledge for all children and youths, practicing a nurturant pedagogy, and ensuring responsible stewardship of the schools. Each part of the mission is based on and permeated by moral dimensions.[4]

Because they perceive all levels of schooling to be intercon-
nected, NNER educators insist that the improvement of the nation's
schools and the improvement of its teacher education programs must
proceed simultaneously. Having better schools requires having better
teachers; preparing better teachers requires having exemplary
schools in which to prepare them. And the word *reform* rarely en-
ters NNER educators' vocabularies: that term implies a finite
process with corruption at one end and completion at the other.
Faculty members at NNER settings prefer to think of educational
improvement as a process of *renewal* by which they continuously
remake good schools and teacher education programs into better
ones through inquiry and hard work. NNER participants work toward the simultaneous renewal of schooling and the education of
educators.

Without a plan, simultaneous renewal would be no more than
a slogan. In other words, it would be morality without efficiency.
The plan, or agenda, by which NNER educators pursue simultaneous renewal has come to be called the Agenda for Education in a
Democracy. No creation of momentary inspiration, the Agenda
emerged over several years as a product of inquiries into schools and
teaching, and it was disseminated by means of several books written or edited by John Goodlad and his associates. Goodlad's *A Place
Called School* (1984) began the process of explicating the Agenda,
and four books published in 1990—*The Moral Dimensions of Teaching, Places Where Teachers Are Taught, Teachers for Our Nation's
Schools,* and *Access to Knowledge*—further developed the essential
concepts.[5] These concepts were clarified for implementation as
nineteen postulates, which describe conditions that must be established in order to achieve the four-part mission for educators and
the schools in which they teach.[6] The postulates guide the efforts
of school and university leaders as they work together to establish
new organizational structures and processes to advance their institutions on the path of simultaneous renewal.

The books in the Agenda for Education in a Democracy series explore key ideas underlying the Agenda and describe strategies for pursuing the simultaneous renewal of schools and the education of educators. *Centers of Pedagogy: New Structures for Educational Renewal* examines a promising configuration for educational improvement—one that brings together in one literal or "virtual" place educators from the schools, teacher education, and the arts and sciences to improve both schooling and teacher preparation. Robert Patterson, Nicholas Michelli, and Arturo Pacheco, each a dean of a school or college of education, present not only the theoretical foundations for centers of pedagogy but also their own personal experiences in attempting to establish such structures. With the other volumes in this series, *Centers of Pedagogy* offers a hopeful narrative of schools and teacher preparation programs as increasingly connected, increasingly moral, and increasingly efficient educational institutions.

TIMOTHY J. MCMANNON
Series Editor
Agenda for Education
in a Democracy

Acknowledgments

The statement "all roads lead to Rome" might well be altered in a simple way to capture the central message of our acknowledgments for this book. For us, all roads lead to John Goodlad. As the contents of the book readily reveal, the concept of a center of pedagogy is almost exclusively his. When the idea began to emerge in his writings, we were fortunate to be located in institutions belonging to the National Network for Educational Renewal (NNER). Such membership afforded us unique opportunities to benefit directly from John's willingness to discuss the concept and to react to our tentative explorations of the idea. His ability to help others understand the importance and value of this organizational construct, coupled with his helpful encouragement to venture forward, gave us the needed support to undertake the experiment.

It is to John that we look as we acknowledge the idea for the book itself. In framing the agenda for the celebrations associated with the fifteenth anniversary of the NNER, he and his colleagues associated with the Institute for Educational Inquiry proposed that one book in the Agenda for Education in a Democracy series focus on centers of pedagogy. The idea interested us, both because we agreed that the topic was worthy of treatment and because we knew that the exercise would help further the development of these important new entities.

Our colleagues in our respective partnerships have been part of the struggle to bring the idea into practice and certainly must be recognized for their important work in that regard. We are grateful to them for their willingness to entertain uncertainty and accompanying frustration in order to test an idea that promised to be the next critical step in the renewal of the education of educators and the schools.

All of our colleagues in the colleges, universities, and P–12 schools that are comprised in the NNER have been steadfast sources of support and have served as examples of educational leaders willing to take risks because of their belief in this work. Their shared vision of providing access to knowledge for all children and preserving and expanding our political and social democracy has sustained us. They have been a network that we have turned to often and that we will continue to turn to in the years ahead.

We are grateful to the many people who have helped in significant ways to make this book possible. In particular, Sharon Black, editor at Brigham Young University, and Timothy J. McMannon, the series editor, worked with us patiently in order to have the book be of one voice.

Bob Patterson thanks in particular his secretary, Karen Eddington, and his wife, Belva Patterson, for their support.

Nick Michelli thanks his wife, Tina Jacobowitz, professor in Montclair State University's Department of Reading and Educational Media, for her wonderful support and understanding in this venture. Nick also thanks Bob Pines for his twenty-eight years of colleagueship and professional inspiration.

Arturo Pacheco thanks especially his wife and colleague, Susana Navarro, executive director of the El Paso Collaborative for Academic Excellence, for her continued professional and personal support.

December 1998   ROBERT S. PATTERSON
                                              NICHOLAS M. MICHELLI
                                              ARTURO PACHECO

About the Sponsor

The National Network for Educational Renewal (NNER) was established in 1986 to put into practice the belief that the improvement of schooling and the renewal of teacher education must proceed simultaneously. In short, good schools require good teachers, and good teachers learn their profession in good schools.

The NNER presently embraces sixteen member settings in fourteen states: California, Colorado, Connecticut, Hawaii, Maine, Missouri, Nebraska, New Jersey, Ohio, South Carolina, Texas, Utah, Washington, and Wyoming. Member settings work to build collaboration among three main groups that play a vital role in the preparation of new teachers: education faculty in colleges and universities; arts and sciences faculty; and faculty in elementary and secondary schools. All told, there are thirty-three colleges or universities, over one hundred school districts, and about five hundred partner schools in the NNER.

The NNER extends the work of the Center for Educational Renewal (CER), which was founded in 1985 by John I. Goodlad, Kenneth A. Sirotnik, and Roger Soder to study and facilitate "the simultaneous renewal of schooling and the education of educators."

To support the work of the NNER and the CER, Goodlad, Soder, and Sirotnik established the independent, nonprofit Institute for Educational Inquiry (IEI) in Seattle in 1992. The IEI oversees leadership training programs for key personnel from NNER settings, administers grants from philanthropic organizations to the NNER, conducts research and evaluation studies, and publishes a series of Work in Progress papers. The IEI is the sponsoring agency for the Agenda for Education in a Democracy series.

About the Authors

The Authors

Robert S. Patterson is dean of the David O. McKay School of Education at Brigham Young University (BYU) and director of the Center for the Improvement of Teacher Education and Schooling at BYU. Prior to joining the faculty at BYU in 1992, he taught at the University of Alberta for twenty-five years, where he also served as dean for eight years. His interests include the history of teacher education and the role of partnerships in educational change.

Nicholas M. Michelli is dean of the College of Education and Human Services at Montclair State University. He provided leadership in launching the nation's first center of pedagogy, joining arts and sciences faculty, teacher educators, and members of the New Jersey Network for Educational Renewal at Montclair State. His interests include critical thinking, school-university partnerships, faculty roles and rewards, and professional development for P–12 and college faculty. He chairs the Governmental Relations Committee of the American Association of Colleges for Teacher Education and works in that role to develop state and federal policy to support the education of educators.

Arturo Pacheco is professor and dean of the College of Education at the University of Texas at El Paso. Prior to coming to El Paso in

1991, he served as assistant vice chancellor at the University of California at Santa Cruz, as a faculty member in the Graduate School of Education at Stanford University, and as associate dean for academic affairs at Stanford. His training is in social and political philosophy and philosophy of education. He is an elected member of the board of directors for the National Board for Professional Teaching Standards and the board of directors for the American Association of Colleges for Teacher Education. He was recently appointed by the governor of Texas to the newly created State Board for Educator Certification.

The Contributors

John I. Goodlad is president of the Institute for Educational Inquiry and codirector of the Center for Educational Renewal at the University of Washington. Throughout his career, he has been involved in an array of educational renewal programs and projects and has engaged in large-scale studies of educational change, schooling, and teacher education. In addition to advancing a comprehensive program of research and development directed to the simultaneous renewal of schooling and teacher education, he is inquiring into the mission of education in a democratic society.

Timothy J. McMannon is a senior associate of the Institute for Educational Inquiry and of the Center for Educational Renewal at the University of Washington and teaches history at colleges and universities in the Seattle area. His main areas of interest include recent U.S. history, the history of American education, and the public purpose of education and schooling.

Centers of Pedagogy

Part I

The Case for Centers of Pedagogy

John Goodlad's concept of a center of pedagogy, introduced in 1990, represented an innovative development in the field of education. The center, if it could accomplish even part of the stewardship Goodlad claimed for it, had the potential to solve or at least reduce some serious problems facing the preparation of teachers and the renewal of schools in the United States.

Educational institutions throughout America had long been struggling with the fragmentation of teacher preparation—the separation of theory, practice, and content for those who were intending to teach. Traditionally, preservice teachers had learned content in the arts and sciences departments of their universities, pedagogical theory in the department or college of education, and practice in a classroom far removed from the university, a setting in which they were often told, "Forget everything you've been taught up there on the hill. Welcome to the real world." Individuals in these three groups—all of whom made significant contributions to the preservice teachers' training—were inclined to minimize the contributions of the others, sometimes making disparaging comments to the students who were struggling to put the input of the three into perspective as they anticipated their careers in teaching. Public school teachers were "uninformed and out of date"; education professors were "unrealistic and out of touch"; arts and sciences professors were "elitist and out of reach." Goodlad proposed a center where these three groups could come together as colleagues, listen to each other, consider each other's positions, appreciate each other's contributions, and work together to create effective programs, projects, policies, structures, and research. Beneath their individual perspectives and differences, all three groups have some common goals, two of the most significant of which are to strengthen teacher preparation and improve public schooling. The center of pedagogy was conceived as a structure to facilitate collaboration in these areas. Some institutions have established centers of pedagogy, some have begun moving toward creating one, and others have at least considered the feasibility of a center for their institution.

The chapters in Part One establish the background and rationale behind centers of pedagogy and examine the historical and contemporary contexts that have influenced the centers' development.

Chapter One demonstrates that what has become the center of pedagogy has roots that reach deep into the history, philosophy, theory, and practice of education in the United States. For half a century, the nation's elementary and secondary schools and its colleges of education have been bombarded by demands for change. Teachers and teacher education have been continually criticized, with varying degrees of viciousness; the P–12 schools and the colleges of education have frequently been pitted against each other, with arts and sciences professors assuming roles that have ranged from catalyst to aggressor. Recently, four significant issues have come to the fore: (1) it is urgent that major improvements be instituted quickly, (2) complex problems and weaknesses require comprehensive changes, (3) collaboration between schools and universities is essential for reforms to be comprehensive and effective, and (4) adding the arts and sciences disciplines to the partnership is important in developing the multifaceted training necessary to prepare teachers, with the center of pedagogy being one way of incorporating this additional unit.

Chapter Two examines the function of school-university partnerships. The collaborative challenges, characteristics, and strategies involved in these partnerships have developed from the roots examined in Chapter One; newly developed centers and centers in process have grown from these structures, nourished by their experiences. The chapter first describes many of the challenges partnerships face in terms of cultures, relationships, perspectives, tensions, and risks. In meeting these challenges, experienced partnerships have developed characteristics and practices that have generated more specific strategies for eventually meeting the challenges and developing units that have been effective in renewing both teacher education and public schooling. Some of these characteristics and strategies are discussed, and examples from actual partnership practice are provided.

Chapter Three examines characteristics and relationships of partnership practice that are important in extending the partnership to a center of pedagogy structure. In addition, it notes enabling conditions that this extension requires, and it raises questions that an institution needs to consider in making decisions about and plans for establishing a center of pedagogy.

1

The Roots of an Idea

The center of pedagogy is a relatively new development in educational change that has emerged primarily in and through the writings of John Goodlad. His book *Teachers for Our Nation's Schools* includes a fable portraying renewal at a "typical university."[1] Central to this renewal process is a new organizational unit that Goodlad calls the "Smith Center of Pedagogy." The allusion in the name is to B. Othanel Smith, whose 1980 treatise, *A Design for a School of Pedagogy*, served as a catalyst for Goodlad's development of the concept.[2]

In the fable, the faculty of the Smith Center includes personnel from what Goodlad describes as "three groups conventionally separated."[3] Faculty from the departments of the arts and sciences that offer majors in teacher education participate, dividing their time between the Center and the typical demands of their academic departments. Faculty from the school of education also accept divided loads, spending about 60 percent of their time in the Center. In addition, teachers from nearby public schools, already in partnership with the college for preparing teachers and researching educational innovations, split their time between teaching classes of children or teenagers and instructing university students. "All . . . share in planning the whole of a program, not a piece of it."[4] The mission of the Center embraces several purposes and functions. Its primary commitment is to "preparing schoolteachers in and for exemplary schools characterized by equity and excellence."[5] In addition, activities are undertaken within the Center that are dedicated to sustaining dialogue, pursuing the Center's agenda, and critiquing and revising what has been undertaken. The Smith Center that Goodlad envisioned oversees university programs and courses, including general studies and enculturation, and provides fieldwork for preservice teachers. It promotes the ongoing structural and curricular school reform that Goodlad refers to as *renewal*, with emphasis on equity in educational opportunities for all students. The development and early function of the Center are not completely smooth or free of controversy, but as one of the characters in the fable concludes, "Education appears to be the one area of human enterprise where we anticipate—indeed, demand—an entirely new model."[6]

The purpose of this book is to move from fable to reality. Major components and operations of the "Smith Center" are being considered, adopted, developed, and refined in a number of sites nationwide. There is a need to bring these ideas, ideals, and experiences together and to give them visibility. Following chapters look at the importance of school-university partnerships, explanations of essential features of centers of pedagogy, descriptions of two centers and one center in process within the National Network for Educational Renewal (NNER), and some consideration of the future of centers of pedagogy.

Taproots from the Past

The concept of the center of pedagogy that B. Othanel Smith foreshadowed in 1980 and John Goodlad proposed in 1990 has roots in earlier proposals for the improvement of teacher education and schooling, proposals that have underscored the need for a new organizational construct in schooling and teacher education. This chapter examines these roots, especially those established since the end of World War II.

Diverse Calls for Reform

As Christopher J. Lucas observes, the body of literature on teacher education "is almost stupefying in its proportions" and includes "literally hundreds of books, published conference proceedings, governmental reports and studies, thousands of articles in professional journals, and specialized newsletters of one kind or another."[7] But although the volume of literature on teacher education reform is extensive, it does not reach consensus on anything except the *need* for reform. In reviewing the vast array of commentary, Lucas notes "deep divisions of opinion and few areas of agreement among the professionals."[8] Others who consider the literature of teacher education and schooling arrive at similarly disheartening conclusions, noting its diversity and the accompanying futility of searching for clear agreement on problems and solutions.

Although they have been abundant and diverse, calls for reform have not been productive. Robert N. Bush concludes from his survey of this vast literature that the "sobering lesson to be learned from the past 50 years of attempted reform of teacher education is that there has been no fundamental reform during that period."[9] From a similar literature review, Seymour Sarason arrives at a similar conclusion: that "it is truly remarkable how cosmetic the changes have been in the preparation of educational personnel." He concludes that the changes are "little more than add-ons to conformity-reinforcing programs."[10]

But not all analysts are this gloomy about the events, movements, and writings of the past. Many are able to see in the past several taproots of ideas and insights that should serve to inform and direct change initiatives emerging in our culture now. The blame they have laid—justified or unjustified—has called attention to educational processes, the participants in educational institutions, and the need for structures that will enable educators to perform their work. Recognition of such needs has been fundamental to the development of centers of pedagogy to assist in the renewal of teacher education and schooling.

Negative Images and Stereotypes

Some of the images and stereotypes that have influenced recent efforts at educational improvement are remarkably similar to ideas that surfaced roughly fifty years ago. In the early post–World War II period, between approximately 1950 and 1965, several writers gained considerable attention for their attacks on schooling and teacher education. Arthur Bestor, a history professor at the University of Illinois, was among the earliest to take aim at the undesirable conditions of public education. His two books, *Educational Wastelands* and *The Restoration of Learning*, blamed the "educationists" responsible for teacher preparation.[11] A graduate of one of the celebrated progressive schools in the nation, the Lincoln School of Teachers College, Columbia University, he argued vigorously against what he judged to be a dangerous trend in education, one he believed to be both anti-intellectual and antidemocratic.[12] He referred to American teacher-training curricula as "the most blatantly vocational and anti-intellectual of all programs."[13] In addition, he attacked the life-adjustment emphasis in the curriculum of the schools and other manifestations of what he referred to as "the cult of contemporaneity," as well as extremes of progressive education. He identified two basic defects in the organization and structure of the educational system: the division "between the public-school world and the world of scholarship, science, and the professions" and "the schism that exists in institutions of higher learning between the professors of pedagogy . . . and all the other faculties."[14] Despite this perceptive analysis of the complexity of the situation, Bestor's solution was simple, and it ignored the divisions he identified. He recommended "a new curriculum for the education of teachers, based firmly upon the liberal arts and sciences, rather than upon the mere vocational skills of pedagogy," which he felt would "do more to restore the repute of the public schools than any other step that can be taken."[15]

Bestor's strident, angry, and uncompromising voice, in concert with the sentiments expressed by other contemporary critics of schooling and teacher education, served more to widen the gap between schools and universities and to deepen the schism within higher education than it did to narrow and heal. Such critics generated stereotypical images of the issues and participants, images that persist in characterizing the problems and personnel in education, even fifty years later. It is not surprising that as some look at the outspoken and somewhat hostile commentary on education and teacher preparation that has surfaced since the publication of A Nation at Risk in 1983, they feel that no significant progress has been made in over half a century. Wayne J. Urban typifies the viewpoint of many, observing that teacher educators of the 1980s were "beset with many of the same problems teacher educators faced for generations."[16]

Significant Developments

Although there are many similarities among the concerns and issues of the early post–World War II era and the concerns and issues of the last two decades of the twentieth century, there are changes and new developments that are more significant than the recurring controversies. Concerned people are recognizing both the urgency of the problems in education and the importance of addressing these long-standing issues in new ways. Laying blame on single groups such as teacher educators and acting in isolated spheres to find solutions are no longer considered adequate.

A study of the literature, along with experience in the enterprise of educational renewal, reveals at least four significant themes in contemporary rhetoric about schooling and teacher education that distinguish recent controversy from that of earlier times:

- A sense of urgency based on indications that educational reform needs to be immediate and consequential

- Widespread recognition that educational changes cannot proceed effectively unless they are comprehensive and recognize the complex nature of the problem

- Acknowledgment that collaborative partnerships involving schools and the whole university are important in effecting needed and desirable change

- The suggestion that centers of pedagogy can provide the organizational construct needed to allow all of the key participants concerned with the preparation of teachers to engage in effective collaboration

A Sense of Urgency

The critics of schooling and teacher education, both fifty years ago and in contemporary times, have touched on a broad spectrum of concerns. Mary Anne Raywid, in her analysis of the period immediately following World War II, observed that virtually no aspect of public education had "gone unquestioned by one source or another."[17] She concluded that American education was "under attack" and that "the practice of criticizing our schools [was] well on its way to becoming a national pastime."[18] Although a brief respite occurred in this heated criticism of public education during the 1970s, the 1983 publication of A Nation at Risk, "an open letter to the American people," set off an extended debate that, as Goodlad observes, "was sustained over three presidencies into a second decade."[19] A veritable avalanche of articles, books, and commissioned reports followed, identifying a variety of ills, offering diverse remedies, and issuing both reasoned and angry demands for action. Politicians at all levels of government, professional educators in every field, and countless others have sought approval and support for their aggressive agendas for reform. In a two-year period from 1983 to 1985, "more than 700 pieces of legislation were enacted in the fifty states to improve the quality of teachers."[20]

"Progress, Productivity and Prosperity"

Although there may seem to be parallels in the heated debates of the 1950s and those of the 1980s, the recent controversies are distinguished by a theme not apparent in the early post–World War II era. The Carnegie Commission's 1986 report, *A Nation Prepared: Teachers for the 21st Century*, identified the condition: "There is a new consensus on the urgency of making our schools once again the engines of progress, productivity and prosperity."[21] Ten years later, in 1996, the authors of *What Matters Most: Teaching for America's Future* also emphasized the urgent need for improving teaching in the nation's schools: "There has been no previous time in history when the success, indeed the survival, of nations and people has been so tightly tied to their ability to learn." Pointing to the obvious needs of the nation for better-educated workers to compete successfully in a global economy, the report highlighted the claim that "America's future depends now, as never before, on our ability to teach."[22] Another observer, Mary Hatwood Futrell, offers a similar perspective. "This nation," she claims, "will not be prepared for the cataclysmic changes and colossal challenges of the 21st century unless teacher educators recommit themselves to finding more effective ways to prepare teachers to prepare future generations to address those changes and challenges."[23]

Social and Lifestyle Preparation

Although many base their urgent calls for renewal of teacher education and schooling on the demands of a competitive economy, there are equally compelling social reasons for this urgency. America is fractured on many planes. Society demands high standards of qualification and performance, but many children lack the parental, community, and school support necessary to develop the competencies they will need. Labeled and discouraged, they fall further and further behind their more privileged peers. Alarming numbers of young people are unable to compete successfully for jobs; the resulting fissure between the haves and the have-nots escalates economic disparity, racial tension, and social alienation. The social-political marring of the nation increases daily in severity and extent. Both the economic and social conditions of the day serve to underscore the urgency of the need to provide quality educational experiences to the young.

Importance of Comprehensive Solutions

A hazard of urgency is that it may focus only on superficial or over-simplified matters. Yet education is neither superficial nor simple. It is a multifaceted, highly complex endeavor that defies simplistic notions of improvement. Unlike reformers such as Bestor and others of his era, critics today realize that correcting a few practices in teacher preparation addresses just one small corner of the problem.

Multiple Issues

Michael Fullan and his colleagues affirm the urgent and complex nature of necessary changes: "There has never been a greater convergence of political and programmatic agreement, energy, and sense of urgency that immediate and sustained action on a comprehensive scale must take place."[24] Alan Tom further develops the point. Speaking critically of colleagues who "continue to believe that the 'problem' of teacher education emanates from a single cause or two," he asserts that "we must resist attempts to reduce teacher education reform to one or two factors." He continues: "Attaining excellence in teacher education is a much more complicated affair than looking solely to the characteristics, beliefs, and work patterns of teacher educators."[25] As someone who has investigated many reform initiatives, Lucas concludes that "if anything had changed" by the last decade of the twentieth century, "perhaps it was the sheer scope and ambition of reform proposals in teacher education emanating from teacher educators themselves."[26]

The scope and ambition of proposed education reforms are farreaching and complex. Daniel Liston and Kenneth Zeichner have studied numerous reports on teacher education, including reports offered by individual teacher educators, organizations, teacher associations, community-wide task forces, and state and federal commissions dating from 1983, when *A Nation at Risk* was published. They conclude that "the reforms for teacher education that have been prepared in all these various reports and proposals vary greatly" and that they show the multiplicity of issues that are addressed by the various observers. Further, Liston and Zeichner observe that these reformers call for changes "in the ways in which prospective teachers are recruited and selected, in the content, organization, structure, and control of preservice and in-service education programs, in the institutional conditions of schooling that facilitate and/or inhibit the work of teachers and other staff, and in the structure and organization of the occupation of teaching."[27]

Interrelated Causes and Solutions

Similar recognition of the broad and complex nature of needed educational improvement is acknowledged in the 1996 report *What Matters Most: Teaching for America's Future*. The report explains that reforms centered on one or two recommended changes are not adequate to meet contemporary needs. As members of the National Commission on Teaching & America's Future, the group responsible for the report, examined the barriers that prevent American schoolchildren from experiencing quality education, they noted the following as factors to be overcome:

1. Low expectations for student performance
2. Unenforced standards for teachers
3. Major flaws in teacher preparation
4. Painfully slipshod teacher recruitment

5. Inadequate induction for beginning teachers
6. Lack of professional development and rewards for knowledge and skill
7. Schools that are structured for failure rather than success[28]

The multifaceted recommendations of this commission offer persuasive testimony to the complexity of current educational needs:

1. Get serious about standards for both students and teachers.
2. Reinvent teacher preparation and professional development.
3. Fix teacher recruitment and put qualified teachers in every classroom.
4. Encourage and reward teacher knowledge and skill.
5. Create schools that are organized for student and teacher success.[29]

The commission concluded, "These ideas must be pursued together—as an entire tapestry that is tightly interwoven."[30]

Thus, educators are recognizing that ideas that at first may seem to compete are actually interrelated within the fabric of change. As Tom affirms, "Unless one concurrently considers normative, structural, personnel, institutional, career, governance, and strategic issues, any effort to reform teacher education will be incomplete and therefore deeply at risk."[31]

Partnerships Between Schools and Universities

During the last years of the twentieth century, there has been continued emphasis on the value of establishing collaborative partnerships in order to achieve renewal of both teacher preparation and public schooling. Three sets of partners are important in this interactive renewal: faculty from the school or college of education, faculty from arts and sciences departments throughout the university, and personnel from local elementary and secondary schools. Although the popularity of such partnerships is a relatively recent trend, precedents for interconnecting these groups can be found in teacher development practices of the past. The groups that are now learning to become partners have moved between open warfare, controlled enmity, and official and unofficial attempts at cooperation. There have been successful movements recently toward the genuine collaborative partnerships that are repeatedly being shown to be necessary for the urgently needed, comprehensive renewal.

"War of the Academic Worlds"

Stinnett observed conditions following the orbiting of the Soviet Union's first *Sputnik*, which prompted such efforts:

> With the near panic of the American people over the prospect of falling behind in the arms and technology race, the schools became easy targets for finger pointing. . . . Everybody in education blamed everybody else. The most convenient scapegoats were the teachers colleges and schools of education, which were attacked by their critics for their alleged easy curricula and poorly prepared teachers. . . . The press, the "slicks," and the TV pundits joined in to heap calumny upon the hapless professors of education, who were accused of fostering anti-intellectualism by turning out teachers who were prepared exclusively in methods courses. The campaign to discredit teacher education reached ludicrous new lows in charges and counter-charges. John Dewey became the great whipping boy and the professors of education the stand-ins. By 1958 the situation was rapidly approaching an impasse, with channels of communication sharply closing, and with the charges growing more

intemperate. These conditions prompted several of the
scholarly societies and professional associations to join in
bringing representatives of the warring groups together.[32]

Writing about this period and these conditions, Hodenfield has
termed this conflict "the war of the academic worlds," pointing out
how "the division between the liberal arts scholars and the teacher
educators erupted in an all-out campaign of invective and vituper-
ation."[33] Arts and sciences professors considered themselves
guardians of knowledge and skills in their respective disciplines; education professors were not capable of teaching the intricacies of
biology, physics, or English literature. But the content-area experts
were not eager to come out of their specialized ivory towers to in-
struct prospective teachers themselves. Assigning blame was easier
than reevaluating turf and constructing new programs.

Movements Toward Peace and Cooperation

Fortunately, not all post–World War II reform attempts exacerbated
the division between the university and the schools or the schism
within the university among professors of the arts and sciences
and those in the school, college, or department of education. There
were those who made the effort to bring teacher education professors and discipline specialists together with school-based personnel
to discuss the improvement of teacher education. Among the voices
encouraging these warring groups to come together was Harold Rugg,
who in 1952 urged university administrators to link education and
liberal arts faculty for design and control of teacher education.
In his view, until such connections were established, "no important
step" could be taken to improve teacher education.[34]

The importance of bridging the gulf separating the key participants in the education of teachers was not totally overlooked. A
major effort was made to engage them in a joint planning activity.
Over a thousand individuals from these disparate groups—teachers,
school administrators, professors of education, discipline scholars,

and administrators of higher education—came together at Bowling Green State University in 1958 with the goal of forming such a connection. This was "the first large-scale national effort to involve representatives of all areas of education from the kindergarten through the graduate school."[35] Tensions were high as the conference opened, with participants and observers skeptical as to whether representatives of these contending factions could set aside their differences and work together. Of the various outcomes of the conference, the most significant was "the virtually unanimous acknowledgment that teacher education is the responsibility of the *entire* college or university."[36] One participant told the conference: "The education of teachers is too important to the nation to be left to the sole jurisdiction of any single group, whether it be composed of professors of education whose central concern has always been for teacher education or of liberal arts professors, many of whom have only recently begun to recognize a long-ignored obligation to help make policy in this area. Teacher education is properly the responsibility of the entire institution."[37]

The prevailing absence of cooperation between scholars in the disciplines and their colleagues in teacher education was highlighted at this conference; further noted was the failure of both groups to become involved in the schools, where they could understand firsthand the world of teachers.

Weak Relationships

Throughout the 1950s and 1960s, professors of education and teachers in the schools generally resented one another. Professors taught theories and espoused new methodologies, telling their students in glowing but abstract terms how teaching could be and ought to be improved. When these students went into the schools for practicum experience, public school teachers welcomed them to the "real world," telling them that professors were simply out of touch with the culture of schools and the needs of children. A decade after the Bowling Green conference, voices were still being raised on the necessity for cooperation between schools and universities. "Teacher education needs help," wrote Melvin W. Barnes. As far as he was concerned, the most serious problems of teacher preparation were "directly traceable to weak relationships between schools and universities."[38] Reporting a study of approximately forty universities, he found "appallingly few instances of substantial school-university cooperation," concluding that "examples of close teamwork between schools and universities are few and far between."[39] Barnes portrayed the relationship (or lack of relationship) between schools and universities in terms of an old Marx Brothers movie in which a lawyer (Groucho) whose office was infested with houseflies expressed the division of labor: "They don't practice law and we don't climb the walls."[40]

Barnes was not alone in his assertion that relationships between schools and universities should be strengthened. One of his colleagues assessed the situation as follows:

A popular view is that the school's responsibility, *the* responsibility, is instruction. . . . I don't really believe this popular view. I think that the school has told itself it has *a* responsibility but that truly it has *two* responsibilities. One is for instruction and the other is for the improvement of instruction. If you will accept this additional assumption, then we've got to abandon the concept of two sovereign nations—the school and the university— joined by some sort of treaty. You know, they get along nicely and they exchange ambassadors and the like. I think that what we really have to look at is the possibility of some concept of overlapping sovereignty.[41]

As time passed, others expressed the importance of school-university relationships. For example, James Bryant Conant suggested clinical professorships and field-based components for teacher education programs,[42] ideas that gained modest acceptance in the

1970s. However, as Alan Tom observed, "These earlier forms of role-based and programmatic collaboration between campus-based professors of education and schoolteachers were never widely implemented."[43]

Collaborative Partnerships

Although these roots were slow in their initial growth, the concept of collaboration for simultaneous renewal has been recognized and nourished until it has become a distinguishing feature of late twentieth-century educational change. Early in the 1980s, John Goodlad began emphasizing the interactive relationship of schools and universities and advocating formal partnerships to promote and advance collaborative initiatives for change. Universities' recognition of the necessary role of schools, and schools' acknowledgment of the importance of teacher education have been, in the opinion of observers like Fullan, "the most salient change" in recent years. Noting "the institution of teacher education reform at or near the head of every agenda for educational rejuvenation," Fullan and others affirm, "A hitherto neglected or subordinate theme has become dominant. Just as it has emerged as a commonplace that reform cannot be achieved without good teachers, so it has become axiomatic that good teachers need and desire a first-class preparation."[44] Thomas Lasley also acknowledges that interdependence must be recognized and promoted, insisting that "the adversarial postures of the past decades" should be discontinued and that "all those directly and indirectly involved in teacher education must begin to think in terms of partnerships."[45] Similarly, Futrell comments that educators must "expand and tighten partnerships" to "help restore the sense of community that America desperately needs if education is to flourish in a context of hopefulness."[46]

Support for and experimentation with partnerships continue. Gene I. Maeroff notes that when he published *School and College: Partnerships in Education* in 1983, "the idea that precollegiate schools and institutions of higher education should cooperate was still a novel notion in some circles," and "voices calling for closer ties between schools and colleges reverberated across a landscape in which often few ears were attuned to hearing them."[47] By 1995, however, approximately twenty-three hundred school-college partnerships existed across the United States.[48] As Maeroff and others have demonstrated, such partnerships have grown not only in numbers but also in acceptance and advocacy.

The reasons given in support of these partnerships in education vary. Some have developed these partnerships to counter the negative effects of adversarial and critical stances that school and university personnel have traditionally taken toward each other's work. Others point to the reciprocal connections between high-quality teacher preparation and high-quality schools. "Few serious-minded people," according to Maeroff, "any longer maintain that issues involving the quality of the teaching force can be addressed on one level while ignoring what happens on other levels."[49]

Agreeing with the importance of partnership, Futrell extends the collaboration between the public school and the school, college, or department of education to include the third of the former combatants: the departments of the arts and sciences. Referring to the separation of P–12 teachers, education professors, and university discipline specialists as "the Berlin wall of the education world," she asserts that the wall should be demolished, creating a new way for parties to relate to each other. In her view, it has become obvious "that education is indivisible and that no part of education can prosper if any part hits bad times."[50] Gerald Tirozzi draws a similar conclusion. "Today," he observes, "university-school partnerships are no longer an anomaly; universities and school districts across the nation are realizing the symbiotic power of partnership."[51]

The complexity of the educational endeavor is now being acknowledged, and proposed renewal initiatives reflect the need for solutions that embrace this complexity. Recognizing the content needs stressed in the Bowling Green conference, collaborative partnerships of university and schools are extending to include participants from other disciplines at the university, especially those that furnish the discipline content of the subject areas of instruction. This form of alliance has not been easy to create or sustain. In many universities and colleges, the faculties of the arts and sciences do not have positive views of teacher education, teacher educators, or public schooling. The earlier outspoken critics, including Bestor, Koerner, Lynd, Rickover, and others, unconditionally blamed poor teachers and deficient schools on so-called educationists in universities. That is, faculty members from other university disciplines have generalized to give teacher education faculty both the classification and the blame. Although trends are changing, human prejudices persist. Structures that have been successful in blending the needs, interests, strengths, and activities of universities and schools need to be reconceived and reorganized to include content-area specialists in the universities as well.

Organizations for Collaborative Action

Given the sense of urgency that is driving educational change, along with the recognition of the complex and comprehensive nature of what is involved and the further understanding that complex needs require cooperation of disparate groups of individuals, many are identifying a fourth major strand in the complex root system of current efforts at renewal: the need for coordinating structures to facilitate collaborative efforts.

Although much of the earlier warfare has subsided into a basic agreement on the need for collaboration, the various participants are different enough to make harmonious association a difficult venture. In responding to the report *What Matters Most: Teaching for America's Future*, Robert Bullough and colleagues explain the difficulty of bringing these groups together within the loosely coupled education community. "Although there is a lot of talk about needing to bring groups together," they note, "the difficulty of bridging school, district, and university cultures is underappreciated." They comment that we seem inclined to assume that district and university personnel will readily establish "widespread, deep agreement and commitment," and that this commitment will be sufficiently strong and compelling to cause the separate groups "to back off from their own agendas, their own commitment, for a greater good."[52] The tendency to cling to one's own agenda and to avoid deep commitment can perhaps be blamed on the superficiality that Zhixin Su says is typical of most partnerships: "Among the large numbers and impressive variety of school-university partnerships . . . too many are best characterized as faddish . . . and some have only been symbolic, 'on-paper' arrangements; or relationships based upon patronage and small monetary grants; or one-sided, noblesse oblige, service arrangements; or information-sharing systems."[53] Such partnerships, Su continues, "focus mostly on piece-meal reform plans" and fail to build strong interinstitutional relationships or to work toward long-term goals to improve education.[54]

That so many school-university partnerships fail to go deeper than commitment to superficial matters may result from the inability of participants to relate to each other's needs and views in more than a superficial way. Lee Teitel sees the challenge as being the need to reorient the personnel of schools and universities so they will be inclined as well as able to work together. The priorities, rewards, and pursuits of the two cultures are so different that a shift in perspective is needed.[55] The respect, openness, and trust necessary to get below the surface in the functions of partnership are dependent on this kind of reorientation. Walter Doyle's examination of teacher education led him to a similar conclusion: "There are powerful centrifugal forces that pull the enterprise of teacher education apart." He remarks that "the epicenter of teacher education lies somewhere between the university and the school systems,"[56] with, as Lucas notes, a "little glue to hold the components together."[57]

Mary Diez presents a similar view, concluding that we still have "a long way to go" in uniting school and university personnel in a common cause and that "concerted institutional efforts will be necessary to create structures that support simultaneous renewal." Like Su, she has noticed a tendency to jump onto the fashionable bandwagon of partnering without recognizing or committing to the challenge of creating the organizational structures necessary to sustain partnerships.[58]

In recent decades, two organizational structures have emerged that have shown great promise for bringing partners together, consolidating their efforts, and helping them develop the perspective required for the kind of selflessness, mutual respect, and trust necessary for simultaneous renewal of teacher education and public schooling. These promising structures are professional development schools and centers of pedagogy.

Professional Development Schools: Experimental Sites

The concept of professional development schools (PDSs) emerged largely through the work of the Holmes Group, an organization of university provosts and deans of education who wanted to bring teacher education into closer synchronization with the needs and realities of the schools. In selected school settings, teacher educators and practicing teachers work collaboratively to strengthen both teacher preparation and public school education. PDSs provide the setting and context for the work of school-university partnerships. The Holmes Group emphasizes that the historical roots of PDSs are in the laboratory schools that colleges and universities formerly maintained as laboratory settings for demonstration, practice, and research. However, the PDS goes beyond the laboratory school to become "an effort to invent an institutional coalition that will bring all the required forces together—universities, schools of education, and public schools."[59] The Holmes Group's report *Tomorrow's Schools* points out that it may be relatively easy to find projects in schools and classrooms in which highly competent and effective administrators and teachers help to create "small islands of the ideal."[60] However, these observers note that it is time to advance beyond these single instances and create communities of inquiry and practice that endure. They look to professional development schools as "an attempt to institutionalize the development of new knowledge and practice so that educators' best ideas are not limited to isolated islands of exemplary practice."[61] According to educators at one of the one hundred universities included in the Holmes Group, successful professional development schools can be identified by three main activities:

- Teachers are afforded the opportunity to take a closer look at their own practice or schoolwide problems and are given time away from the classroom to work on these issues.

- Teachers and administrators in the school are centrally involved in the preparation of preservice teachers.

- These schools have a dissemination responsibility. What is learned in these schools must be made available to as wide a network of educators as possible.[62]

Although professional development schools have been a means of systematically extending ideas for improvement throughout schools and universities, some observers note that they have fallen short of the ideal. Andy Hargreaves states the problem with an analogy, writing of the need to transform islands of excellence into archipelagoes. The challenge, as he expresses it, is to make the professional development school part of a larger, more inclusive renewal effort.[63] Fullan and colleagues state a similar position in reviewing the ten-year history of the Holmes Group: "The influence of the PDS on other schools in the district, changes in the colleges of education's overall teacher preparation programs, and transforming incentives and the culture of the college as an institution all remain problematic."[64] Widespread efforts to establish professional development schools have been both evidence of the popularity of the idea and targets for criticism of it. The professional development school has now "become a commonplace of the discourse of reform," write Fullan and his coauthors, "so much so that there is a lurking danger of 'PDS' becoming a vacuous mantra rather than a carefully specified regime of reform."[65] Part of the inconsistency in reception of the PDS may be, as Zimpher notes, that these schools "exist in great variation" and "often without the direct and sustaining support of the college as a whole or the school district." She concludes that as a result, "PDSs need to be situated in the institutional context such that the daily decisions of the organizations they serve protect their continuing development."[66]

Centers of Pedagogy: "Proofing Sites"

The strengths and weaknesses of professional development schools as structures to support the renewing efforts of school-university partnerships have led to the development of centers of pedagogy. Goodlad's fable of the Smith Center of Pedagogy introduces the concept of such a structure and gives it a visible, if hypothetical, form. Such a center provides a stronger, more stable organization to deal with the challenge of uniting public schools, schools or colleges of education, and academic disciplines across the university in collaborative efforts to renew teacher preparation and schooling.

Goodlad proposes that a center of pedagogy offers ways to deal with several of the problems that he believes undermine quality teacher preparation and schooling: an underfunded mandate to prepare teachers, a lack of shared commitment to the endeavor, a failure to ensure the involvement of all three of the entities that must collaborate to improve teacher preparation and schooling, and a lack of agreement on and pursuit of a common set of ethical and moral purposes to form the basis for policy and operation as well as curricula of the school.[67] A review of the literature shows the attention Goodlad's idea has attracted in recent years. But although several commentators see merit in the idea, they tend to agree with Tom's claim that the concept "must be considered to be an ideal type because very few such units have been created" and because the details about how "to create, organize, and sustain a center for pedagogy" remain vague and largely untried. To Tom, "the internal workings of the center are hazy"; nevertheless, he calls the center of pedagogy "an idea of considerable interest."[68] Those who are developing and experimenting with such centers agree that the idea has merit. It addresses the need to create an organizational construct to enable complex renewal to occur through the combined efforts of school personnel, education professors, and colleagues in academic areas throughout the university.

Other observers likewise consider Goodlad's presentation of the center of pedagogy to be meritorious in theory but hazy in application. They need to look beyond the fact that Goodlad is not positioned in an institution where he is able to create a center of pedagogy to other institutions that, influenced and guided by Goodlad, are in various phases of applying the concept. Through the NNER, Goodlad is connected to sixteen school-university partnerships across the United States. Using a metaphor originally employed by Phyllis Edmundson, Goodlad refers to the NNER settings as "proofing sites": places where ideas, like the yeast in bread dough, are activated by conditions of schools and universities working together.[69] Goodlad and his associates at the Center for Educational Renewal and the Institute for Educational Inquiry have provided ideas, guidance, resources, and encouragement to these varied sites, some of which have been affiliated with the NNER since its inception in 1986.

The work of these partnership "proofing sites" has progressed through a series of stages. In most cases, they began with building and sustaining collaborative partnerships between public schools and schools or colleges of education. Eventually their collaboration led to establishing partner or professional development schools. Gradually they refined their agendas through examining and applying Goodlad's nineteen postulates as a framework for pursuing simultaneous renewal of schooling and teacher education. In the course of these activities, they expanded their collaborative efforts by including colleagues from the departments of the arts and sciences.

As Goodlad began writing about the concept of a center of pedagogy, some of the sites in the NNER began establishing such centers and exploring their potential as constructs for organizing and facilitating collaborative work. These centers are currently in various phases of development and experimentation. The NNER settings nationwide represent a variety of circumstances and forms of collaboration: Some include one university, some several; some universities are public, some private; some include only a few school districts, others are statewide consortia; some universities prepare fewer than a hundred teachers a year, others over a thousand. As the settings are unique, it is only reasonable to expect that the centers of pedagogy will be unique as well. In the midst of diversity, however, there are common characteristics that constitute the core of the idea.

The following chapters provide an understanding of the centrality of school-university partnerships to the establishment of centers of pedagogy, establish a clearer definition of these centers, and describe three fledgling efforts to establish these centers. The concluding chapters look at the expanding interest in this organizational construct and its future possibilities.

2

Operating Effective School-University Partnerships

Conceptually and operationally, centers of pedagogy are extensions of the effective operation of school-university partnerships. These partnerships are characterized by the overlapping sovereignty that links such collaborative institutions, and they illustrate the point developed in Chapter One that it is very difficult to bridge the gap between school and university.

The increase in numbers, types, and commitments of partnerships has been well documented. But despite partnerships' growth and centrality to the work of schools and universities, administrators are just beginning to understand the processes of working across the traditional boundaries of these entities. According to Theodore Gross, collaborative partnerships have reached a watershed point in their history, where they "must become more than marginal to our educational institutions."[1]

As educators call for increased school-university collaboration, they simultaneously express concern about how poorly the process is understood.[2] Some authors have pointed out that "collaboration is not easy to achieve"[3] and that it remains an elusive concept to many who have tried to engage in it. Collaborative partnership participation by school and university personnel is, as Mary Christenson and colleagues recognize, "more than just talking and working together, and it is more complicated than simply 'bridging the differences' that separate schools and universities." They see it as a matter of altering relationships, a means of "significant and lasting personal growth" that may "lead to substantial organizational change."[4] Undoubtedly both the demanding nature of the process and its potential ramifications for altering existing practices are among the reasons that the concept of effective collaborative partnership is just beginning to be understood.

Another reason that school-university partnerships are not well understood is that the day-to-day operation of such arrangements has not been well documented. Those who advocate and participate in these collaborations, according to McGowan and Powell, "rarely analyze their operation, assess their effectiveness, or indicate guidelines for their effective implementation."[5] Other authors cite observers who note that "evidence of successful school-university collaboration is spotty at best" and that few participants "present either information about the initiation or maintenance of the collaboration or empirical evidence of program effectiveness."[6] Winitzky, Stoddart, and O'Keefe express a similar viewpoint: "Although partnerships have often been advocated, the literature is quite limited. We know little about what works, what does not, and why."[7]

In response to this need for a greater understanding of successful partnership practice, this chapter examines the challenges of creating a successful collaborative relationship between universities and public schools, identifies and discusses elements that contribute to effective collaboration, and examines some ways in which partners can create an organization capable of resisting the forces that tend to separate the school-university unit. Because a center of pedagogy has the capability to become such an organization, examining these challenges will reveal considerations relevant to establishing and operating such a center.

Challenges of Collaboration

The literature that does exist on effective collaborations in school-university partnerships, along with the experiences of successful partnerships at Montclair State University in New Jersey, Brigham

Young University in Utah, and the University of Texas at El Paso, reveals a number of challenges that must be recognized, understood, and dealt with if successful partnerships are to be established:

- The deeply rooted cultures of both schools and universities result in indifferent or adversarial relationships with each other. These cultures are highly resistant to change.

- Collaboration is hard work, requiring persistent effort, patient resolving of differences, and a rigorous schedule of planning, implementation, and study.

- The benefits of collaboration may not be immediately apparent; participants must approach the partnership from a long-term perspective.

- Participants must regard partnerships as organic and generative. Partnerships tend to be messy because they are appreciably different in nature and function from the organizations of which they are composed; their focus is usually pragmatic, and partners are continually adjusting, adapting, and responding to circumstances.

- Tensions are an inevitable product of messy relationships; depending on how they are handled, such tensions may produce either dysfunction or positive energy.

- Although hundreds of school-university partnerships exist, little has been written describing effective operation. New partnerships find little to inform their establishment and function.

- Because partnerships are demanding and multidimensional, and because they lack long-term models or an extensive knowledge base, they are high-risk ventures, characterized by frustration and a tendency toward failure.

When these challenges are not recognized and understood, they can become major impediments to the successful development and sustained operation of collaborative work. Each warrants more specific examination and development.

Tradition-Bound Cultures

One wit has observed that universities are slower and more difficult to move than cemeteries. Although schools may seem a little less ponderous and are perceived to engage in frequent innovative and experimental projects, they too tend to resist change in the ways that they operate and provide services to their students. When two such tradition-bound institutions join together in ventures aimed at renewing the operations of both of them, their intractability can become both glaringly apparent and restrictive. Coombs and Hansen refer to this phenomenon as the "tenacity of tradition." Their study of secondary school teachers and university professors revealed that both groups "hesitated to break with tradition and resisted trying something new."[8] Not only are the cultural values of these organizations deeply entrenched, but they are also often quite different, even working at cross-purposes.[9]

When school and university people first attempt to work out a collaborative relationship, they tend to keep testing each other to see whether the commitment to working together is sincere. In one such partnership, members of one of the university's foreign language departments attempted to collaborate with several high school teachers. The high school teachers, suspecting that the college faculty might not really be willing to give up some of their traditional turf in spite of their outward commitment to collaboration, asked for a concession that had been refused repeatedly in the past. They wanted to be able to teach college-level courses in the high school, for which their students would receive credit under a "concurrent enrollment" plan. This request challenged the university's culture, which maintained that college-level courses needed to be taught by college-employed teachers. Although allowing this change was a challenge to their way of thinking, the college professors agreed, thus demonstrating that they were willing to reconsider matters of their culture in order to achieve and benefit from the collaboration.

Demanding Relationships

Brookhart and Loadman point out that overcoming the different cultural foci of institutions takes "commitment and hard work."[10] Those who undertake this sharing and negotiating process often fail to anticipate just how demanding collaborative relationships can be. In examining new roles that must be created in partnerships, Sandholtz and Finan cite a comment from one of the partnership participants, a woman they identify as Judith: "Time and again over the years, I have been reminded that true collaboration is hard work. . . . Even the simple task of setting times and places for meetings often becomes complex. Moreover the amount of time needed for collaborative activities is invariably underestimated. I'll admit to more than one occasion when I have thought it would be much easier to work alone."[11] Ultimately in favor of collaboration, Judith further commented, "Although I periodically decry the incredible amount of time and energy required for collaboration, I firmly believe the results are better."[12]

Judith's assessment is consistent with the findings of Lasley, Matczynski, and Williams, who identified three distinguishing characteristics of collaborative projects, the second of which was "high work intensity."[13] They found that overcoming barriers created by the differences in the ways cultures work and relate to each other required many meetings and extensive conversation. Similarly, Torres-Guzman and her colleagues concluded from their study of differences in collaboration that processes are both complicated and difficult.[14]

Long-Term Perspective

When partnership participants recognize the difficulty of merging different cultures in a work-intensive relationship, it becomes evident that to expect significant results immediately would be unreasonable.

As Sidney Trubowitz observes, "To expect the quick panacea is to fail to recognize that we are working on problems with long histories and that patience is needed to deal with the causes."[15] One might add parenthetically, "and with the processes." Others confirm the need for a long-term perspective. Working in a school-university partnership, according to Coombs and Hansen, is demanding. They note that if partnerships are to be successful, participants need to allow "sufficient time for planning, cooperation, implementation, assessment, and adaptation."[16]

Pragmatic, "Messy" Organizations

In their review of school-university collaborations, McGowan and Powell point out that such organizations have a capacity to "self organize."[17] In other words, participants who are pursuing common goals need to be responsive to new situations and capable of dealing with them. For example, in one of the partnerships in the National Network for Educational Renewal (NNER), conditions arising from growth within the partnership have naturally generated communication structures and opportunities. Early in the partnership's history, an annual conference was the principal means of communicating and sharing. As the partnership continued to grow and expand its operation, needs emerged that could not be addressed adequately at the annual conference. School and university colleagues began to express their frustration over their inability to find time to consider new programs and activities that were occurring throughout the partnership, which included five school districts in addition to the university.

As a result, linking conferences were instituted, whereby participants from all five districts joined periodically in a series of meetings to share and compare innovations and to discuss topics relevant to partnership function, teacher preparation, and school renewal. As the number of professional development schools within the districts increased and the projects became more varied and complex, district conferences were instituted to focus on the specific needs and happenings within each district. The experience of this partnership shows that when collaboratives are flexible and open to consideration of all participants' needs, the messiness that may be generated by growing pains and individual desires can open avenues that improve partnership operation.

Inevitable Tensions

Lyons, Stroble, and Fischetti concur that collaboratives are characterized by inventiveness, flexibility, and fluidity, but note that these very characteristics "can create tensions" and that the adaptations that partners have to make as a result of collaborative agreements "can place stress on the institutions and their members."[18] Bascia agrees that participants in partnerships must expect "unavoidable conflicts" and extends the point by insisting that partners must develop skills and attitudes requisite for working through them.[19] Osguthorpe and Patterson agree that partners need to learn to deal with tension; they warn that if tensions are seen as "insurmountable obstacles," participants may withdraw before the change process is accomplished. They suggest that tensions be viewed as "positive stimulants to change rather than as hindrances."[20]

Participants in one university–public school partnership undertook a complete restructuring of the elementary education program at the university, reorganizing sequences, realigning courses, and arranging for preservice teachers to spend two semesters as members of cohorts in elementary classrooms, taking their methods courses on site before beginning their traditional student teaching experience. The entire elementary education faculty of the university, representatives from arts and sciences courses across campus, teachers and administrators from public schools, and representative university students met several days a week for six weeks to hammer out the necessary changes. Tensions surfaced almost daily: professors teaching methods courses in literacy and mathematics had to surrender some of their credit hours to increase course offerings in music, art, and drama; school personnel proclaimed that some of the professors' favorite ideas would put heavy stress on and increase the workloads of the classroom teachers who would provide practice opportunities and supervision for the cohort students; and the students pointed out that parts of the proposed program would put unrealistic demands on future students. There were times when participants' voices became hard and defensive—even a few times when low but audible disparaging comments were made as soon as a particularly opinionated person left the room. There were also sincere apologies, opportunities for all participants to express their positions and listen to the positions of others, and a number of activities, both planned and spontaneous, that enabled the disparate group members to create together and laugh together. Three years later, those who participated looked back on the experience as a series of opportunities to extend themselves and to grow. Out of tensions came energy, creativity, collegial understanding, and personal growth. The resulting restructured elementary education program has been acknowledged as difficult but very effective by all participants, especially the students who have graduated from it and found that it has prepared them well for their professional work in the schools.

Tensions in partnership work are inevitable and challenging. But if mutual trust and respect override momentary disagreements and frustrations, tensions can generate energy and creativity, ultimately drawing the partners closer together as everyone's performance is challenged and improved.

Uncharted Territory

Although partnerships have increased in number and type and are accepted widely in the education rhetoric of the 1990s, in many ways they are uncharted territory. Even those who promote them and participate in them find them risky and unpredictable. The reasons for this prevailing uncertainty vary, but the main causes seem to stem from the limited number of quality partnerships that have been documented over an extended time and from the lack of systematic inquiry into their nature and operation. Only recently have

there been attempts to build a body of knowledge to inform implementation, growth, and development of these collaborative structures. Sharon Robinson and Linda Darling-Hammond encourage
those engaged in collaborative endeavors such as professional development schools "to document the experience of collaboration
for reflection and learning."[21] Although the encouragement is strong
and the benefits obvious, few collaborators find the time or the resources to provide systematic records of activities, challenges, and
success or failures of partnership activity; the work of partnerships
is so demanding that documentation and record keeping are often
neglected. The few books, book chapters, and journal articles that
have been written on the ups and downs of partnership experience
(including this book) only begin to meet this significant need.

Risks and Uncertainties

The combined effects of these challenges make collaboration, in
the words of Robinson and Darling-Hammond, a matter of "risk,
consternation, and frequent failure."[22] Until the challenges are better understood and the processes and outcomes of successful partnerships more clearly documented, new partnership attempts will
often be haunted by suspicions, negative attitudes, and fears of failure. Still, as Robinson and Darling-Hammond affirm, partnerships
are "an imperative of professional responsibility in education."[23]

Elements of Effective Collaboration

From what has been documented of effective collaboration between schools and universities, a number of common factors are
beginning to emerge. Most who have written about positive partnership experiences have noted that mutual trust is essential. Many
explain that trusting relationships must be built on open, honest
communication. When lines of communication are open, partners
are able to identify and commit to common goals, enabling them
to recognize that in promoting and enriching the work of their

partners, they are promoting and enriching aspects of their own work as well.

Because partnerships are pragmatic, they must have a strong but flexible governance structure—one that provides necessary systems through which goals can be determined and achieved. This governance must be dynamic and adaptable, allowing adequate voice and resources for all participants. The unpredictability and messiness of partnerships demand that nothing be ironclad or immovable. Also necessitated by the messiness are ways of managing and balancing the inevitable pressures, turning them whenever possible into positive tensions. Finally, the factors of flexible governance and positive tensions emerge from, and in turn must be allowed to promote, a culture of inquiry. Such inquiry includes a commitment to study the nature of the collaborative endeavor itself—its issues, activities, and outcomes—in addition to all aspects of teacher preparation and school renewal that are relevant to and viable within the partnership's domains.

Mutual Trust

In their article on school-university partnerships, Sandholtz and Finan report four main lessons they learned about cultivating trust in collaborative relationships. First, they say that attention needs to be given to developing relationships, not just to implementing programs. They observe that when the program director spent time conversing with colleagues, barriers were overcome and school personnel became less suspicious about her reasons for being in their school. Second, they find that trust increases as people see their ideas accepted and implemented. Traditionally, the ideas of teachers had not been given status equal to those of the administrators and university personnel. As teachers saw their proposals being given consideration by the others, they came to view both their own contributions and their relationships with their university colleagues differently. Third, Sandholtz and Finan recognize that trust develops when both individuals and institutions benefit from the partnership. Finally, they find that trust grows as increasing numbers of people become directly involved with partnership activity. Heightened involvement produces a wider range of activities, an increased responsiveness to varying interests and needs, and greater understanding and support for all participants.[24]

Similarly, Coombs and Hansen observed the importance and effects of trust in a partnership between university and secondary school personnel. When they tried to extend partnership activity beyond the administrative level, they found some secondary teachers to be resentful toward university professors and some professors to be patronizing toward secondary teachers. "Before serious partnership activities can be developed," they concluded, "a trusting and equitable atmosphere must be developed among all participants."[25]

Honest Communication

Open, honest communication results from and contributes to trusting relationships. Collaborations are destined to fail if participants feel that they cannot express freely and openly what is on their minds. Robinson and Darling-Hammond point out that "open dialogue . . . allows colleagues to recognize each other's strengths and needs so that professional collaboration can occur and supportive norms can be established."[26]

One does have to be careful that such discourse is not misunderstood or misinterpreted, however. A dean of a college of education was visiting a partner school following its first year of collaboration in a new teacher education program. Shortly into the meeting, the teachers in the school began voicing a number of their concerns about aspects of the program that had not worked well and practices that they thought needed to be changed. The dean listened with mixed feelings of disappointment, frustration, and even anger. Finally, he proposed to the group that if the problems were so extensive, perhaps the school should no longer participate in the program. The teachers who had been expressing their concerns were quite surprised by the suggestion. Realizing that they had been misunderstood, they quickly explained that they definitely wanted to continue the relationship. They described some earlier, less positive experiences with the university and remarked that under this new program they felt trusted and valued by university personnel. Because they felt that their input was important, they were willing to speak freely and openly about the experience. Their desire had been to participate in improving the program, not to terminate their participation in it. What might have been a negative encounter turned into an affirmation of the positive relationship the teachers felt with the university. They felt that the relationship was strong enough to withstand frank and open discussion.

Common Goals

It is possible to engage in a form of partnership based on even shallow or very limited common ground. Often unlikely partners join forces as a necessary expediency to achieve an end that both value for different reasons. Partnerships based on pragmatic grounds are like political alliances in which traditional opponents unite to defeat an initiative because they share a belief that it is wrong but have different proposals to offer in place of it once the defeat has been achieved. Partnerships formed for short-term expediency do not last, unless during the course of operation the participants are able to find a broader base of common interest and frame new goals reflecting greater shared values.

From examining two professional development schools, Lyons, Stroble, and Fischetti concluded, "Lack of a shared commitment, for whatever reason, can radically affect what can be achieved. Shared visions and commitments are critical."[27] Further, they explain, "Without a shared vision of what students could be, especially intellectually, and what teachers need to do, reform will not be sustained within either [schools or teacher education programs]."[28] Studies currently being done in Australia also agree on the importance of shared vision to successful collaboration.[29]

For example, a shared goal of getting educators-in-training out of campus classrooms and into the schools as much as possible has long guided activities and projects in one well-established school-university partnership. Prospective principals spend most of their preparation program in extended internships in public schools, serving as administrators at the elementary, middle, and high school levels. Prospective elementary teachers must spend forty hours in classrooms observing and assisting and must reflect on and analyze their experience before they are even considered for admission to the teacher preparation program. Once accepted, these students spend two semesters in intensive school practicums as they take their methods courses; then they complete the traditional one-semester student teaching assignment or a one-year internship during which they teach their own classes and receive half of a teacher's salary for doing so. Under a program that is currently proving very successful, preservice interns are participating in a junior high school experiment in which they work full time with teams consisting of regular education teachers and special education teachers to create a "school within a school" in which students with behavioral disorders are integrated full-day into classrooms with peers without disabilities. These interns participate in team planning and in a variety of aspects of student and teacher support. All of these programs demand intensive participation by school personnel in addition to great time and energy on the part of university supervisors. The shared goal of getting preservice educators into the schools so that they can apply the theory that they are learning at the university to the context of daily school practice is important enough to members of this partnership that all groups are willing to make the sacrifices required.

According to Robinson and Darling-Hammond, "A strong consensus regarding the outcome, a vision of the new organization to be created, and the mission of that organization" are critical to the ability to resolve differences and approach new issues that will inevitably arise in collaborative arrangements.[30] Agreement on mutual goals is not something that is established just once; such agreement must be revisited and refined again and again. Through discussion, argument, and debate, purposes will become clearer and meaning will be extended; misunderstandings will be reduced at a root level. If the values framework is in place, and adapted and adjusted when appropriate, differences that arise among partners will likely be matters of strategy and instrumentality rather than of ends and principles. Such external differences are generally much easier to resolve than those that may go back to questions relating to foundational beliefs and values.

The partnership mentioned earlier that stressed preservice participation in the schools is now in the process of restructuring its secondary education program. Much negotiation is occurring between secondary education professors at the university and secondary teachers in the partnership school district. There is no question of whether the new program will take cohorts into the schools; the issues to be resolved center on how the program will be administered. As long as all partners agree on the common goal of in-school participation, the external issues can and will be resolved.

Flexible Governance

Many observers of partnerships acknowledge the importance of creating and maintaining an organizational structure that ensures representation of all partner constituencies and is responsive to changing conditions. Trubowitz, for example, identifies as a feature of successful partnerships a "governance structure which allows for as broad a representation as possible" and ensures "varied input and a broad sense of ownership."[31] Smith affirms this importance. Her study of nearly forty award-winning collaborative programs revealed the frequency of change within these successful programs and stressed the corresponding importance of "some type of governing structure" that would adequately represent the partners.[32]

In a partnership that has been sustained for more than twelve years, a governing board that includes leaders from each partner group has remained an anchor for the partnership's shared goals and for the continued commitment of its members. The dean of the college of education of the participating university has changed four times during the life of the partnership, and the superintendents of the participating school districts have all changed at least once. In spite of this complete turnover of the governing board members, none of the partners has wavered in activity or participation, because consistency in goals, values, and policies was established early in the partnership's existence.

Much expansion and many changes have occurred as the partnership has developed and matured, and organizational flexibility has been required. Several structures and systems—such as task forces, ad hoc committees, standing committees, and a coordinating council—have emerged, functioned, and been discontinued when changes have been appropriate. Recently a center of pedagogy has been created to provide a whole new set of structures, councils, committees, and procedures to provide governance and guidance to an ever-expanding scope of partnership operation. These new structures provide new means for addressing problems, resolving differences, substantiating commitment, and voicing both common and differing perspectives. Though a seeming irony, it is the ability to change in response to change that has contributed a good deal of the stability and endurance that the partnership has maintained.

Positive Tensions

With varying reward systems, work schedules, purposes, role definitions, and institutional values, members of a school-university partnership cannot escape tensions as they attempt to work together. Lyons, Stroble, and Fischetti confirm this inevitability with their observation that partner relationships are "not without dilemmas, tensions, and critical questions." However, these researchers do not advise that partnership participants ask how to reduce the tensions; they suggest that partners ask "how they can be sustained."[33] If members of a partnership emphasize fluidity, invention, new relationships, and shared vision, tensions become an important by-product of their existence.

Osguthorpe and Patterson focus on understanding and relating to tension by identifying specific areas of strain, including membership, role definition, planning, and evaluation. For each tension, they note that extremes will exist; they emphasize finding a balance point that captures the best aspects of both extremes—a point at which each tension can be turned into a beneficial effect.[34]

A Culture of Inquiry

Conventional wisdom governs much of what is done in the name of education in schools as well as in universities. To rely on research to gain understanding and alter practice is not common among education professionals. Thus, change tends to be minimal and narrowly conceived. Lieberman argues that if teachers (and, we should add, professors) are open to changing their practice in order to improve it, they "must have opportunities to discuss, think about, try out, and hone new practices" and that an important way to achieve such an outcome is "by creating a culture of inquiry, wherein professional learning is expected, sought after, and an ongoing part of teaching and school life."[35] Kimball and McClellan argued in favor of this same point in the early 1960s: "No longer can casual, informal processes of learning enable an adult to change his thought and action in response to the changes occurring around him. Not only is change too rapid for this gradual process; it is also too deep and penetrates too many aspects of life to permit an adequate adjustment by untutored trial and error."[36]

Certainly this need for change to be informed by reliable research is especially important for educators. With the multiplicity of factors that affect teaching and learning today, educators must engage in systematic study of conditions and behaviors that can contribute significantly to improvement. Otherwise, any change that occurs, favorable or unfavorable, will be on the part of individuals rather than institutions and thus will be severely limited in scope.

At a large school-university partnership that emphasizes inquiry, teachers and administrators in the participating school districts identified literacy as a key area in which they wanted to make some important changes, with a balanced literacy approach as an area of particular interest. Arrangements have been made by the partnership for university and school teachers to engage together in extensive study, and opportunities are being provided for some of the participants to travel to New Zealand to observe balanced literacy practices that have been successful over many years.

In the field of science, of course, new discoveries are continually changing the ways science is practiced and the ways that it must be taught. At one multifaceted partnership, participants from the university's college of education and departments of science and mathematics joined with P–12 teachers in a number of school districts and with practicing scientists in the area to initiate a series of summer institutes in which teachers engaged in extensive study of methodology while they participated with children in field projects involving wetlands, fossils, recycling, and other studies of special interest to the groups. When the schoolteachers returned to their classrooms, they initiated experiential projects that they had designed and committed to during the summer institute. Their innovative ways of teaching science have made these teachers a positive influence in their schools and districts, as well as in their individual classrooms.

Strategies for Establishing Effective Collaborations

A number of specific strategies seem to form a basis for operating successful, long-term partnerships. Prominent among these strategies are the following:

- Design and undertake one or two specific projects that will demonstrate the value of collaborating and test the compatibility of the partners.

- Define and establish new roles that bridge the cultures represented in the collaborative activities.

- Set realistic expectations and perspectives.

- Identify rewards of significance to the participants, and make sure that equivalent rewards are available for both university and school personnel.

- Arrange frequent opportunities for sharing and discussing, opportunities that encourage partners to listen to one another and to respect each other's input and experience.

The Value of Projects

Not all individuals, groups, or institutions are capable of making the necessary sacrifices or of changing behavior sufficiently to work in effective collaborative relationships. Some have the ability but not the readiness. If groups of people who are uncertain about partnership work are given the opportunity to begin collaborating on a limited basis on a specific, well-focused project, they may be able to discover the value of cooperating in this manner and gain a few skills for meeting the demands of such relationships.

Early in the development of one of the NNER partnerships, task forces were formed to draw university and public school personnel into projects that would get them immediately involved in collaborative relationships. The gifted/talented task force, one of the earliest and most active of these groups, drew faculty from throughout the university into projects in which they designed curriculum units to be distributed to teachers throughout the partnership. When a collection of artifacts from the time of Ramses II was exhibited at the university, the collaborative task force drew in historians and archaeologists from the university to design and publish materials that would prepare children with the background necessary to understand and appreciate artifacts in the display. Preservice teachers prepared activities and visual aids to motivate the children and went into the schools to give presentations to many classes. Thousands of children visited the exhibit with the knowledge base to understand how the objects they were seeing fit into the context of life in early Egypt and the actions of Ramses as ruler. Guides at the exhibit were often amused to hear young children teaching their parents as they viewed the artifacts together.

The success of the Ramses project was so gratifying that the task force drew in other cross-campus faculty for additional curriculum projects. During an Olympic year, for example, faculty from the college of education, the public schools, and the college of physical education, with some participation from colleagues in the sciences, put together a packet on the Olympics. In another case, using supporting material from the National Aeronautics and Space Administration, many faculty members in the sciences joined with education and public school personnel to produce an extensive gifted/talented packet on space flights. In yet another project, faculty from visual arts, music, drama, and dance, in addition to administrators from the university's fine arts museum, collaborated with university and public school personnel to prepare curricula for introducing children to a variety of aspects of the humanities and arts, preparing them for visiting various exhibitions scheduled and anticipated for the museum. This collaborative project was extended to create a tradition of Saturday workshops and activities at the museum in which children engage in hands-on experiences with the arts in conjunction with various features and exhibitions. Artists from throughout the region, as well as fine arts professors from the university and teachers from the schools, participate in these projects.

Through the collaborative curriculum units and activities of the gifted/talented task force, the relationship of college of education faculty and public school teachers and administrators concerned with gifted/talented education has become strong. In addition, cross-campus departments and groups that would have been hesitant to commit to long-term collaborative relationships with either the college of education or the public schools were willing to involve themselves in temporary projects. For some units, such as the college of physical education, the collaboration did not last beyond a single project. But for other groups, including the departments in the college of fine arts, the collaboration has become a continuing relationship. Departments of the visual arts, music, drama, and dance have developed courses in classroom applications of their fields. These courses are required in and contribute significantly to the university's teacher preparation program.

The Benefit of New Roles

As the experiences of the fine arts faculty and the gifted/talented task force show, once individuals from varying cultures begin to participate in a collaborative project, they assume new roles, and sometimes they find these roles exhilarating. In fact, one of the university dance instructors who worked in collaborative projects with this partnership became so interested in elementary teaching that she enrolled in the elementary teacher preparation program to obtain teacher certification. The bridge that she created, though a bit unusual, enabled her colleagues in fine arts to view the cultures of P–12 schools and teacher education with more interest and less suspicion than in the past. One of the education professors with a specialty in technology, who had once participated on a collaborative committee with this dance teacher, heard about her enrollment in teacher education and asked permission to do a multimedia case study on her experience. The cultures of a technology specialist and a dance professional are certainly different, but the compatible working relationship of these two individuals demonstrates to the entire partnership that individual cultures can and should be beneficially crossed.

Despite differences in language, priorities, and styles of communication and interaction, separate cultures can meld into constructive, collaborative relationships when individuals have the motivation and the courage to do so. The unique participation of the dance instructor and the education technology expert happened spontaneously. However, Trubowitz suggests that partnerships should deliberately assign "a person who is familiar with both the university and public school cultures to work full time as a university liaison."[37]

Several authorities on partnering have commented on the value of creating and supporting new roles for school and university personnel, new positions that incorporate aspects of both cultures into new responsibilities. Sandholtz and Finan choose the term *boundary spanners* for those important individuals "who understand the dynamics and cultures of both worlds [and] are vital in linking schools and universities in viable collaboration."[38] Both of these authors—one from a university and one from a public school—functioned in cross-institutional roles. In doing so, they discovered the value of these new roles. In several instances they helped to prevent problems, improve planning, and foster collaborative efforts because they could move freely between the school and university and thus translate the culture of each to the other.

Some of the partnerships highlighted in this book have been successful in creating boundary-spanning roles. For example, one university college of education created the position of clinical faculty associate to enable public school teachers to be released from their regular classroom duties for two years to devote their time to supervising student teachers and working with the partner schools of their districts. They are considered adjunct faculty of the university and are given assistance to pursue graduate programs as well. Having spent many years in the public schools, they are members of the school culture; functioning with the university faculty—attending meetings, planning sessions, retreats, and the like—they are immersed in the university culture as well. They become bicultural—able to comprehend and translate aspects of both cultures that might cause confusion or misinterpretation. School colleagues are willing to confide in them regarding matters that they might be embarrassed or intimidated to take to university representatives. Where clinical faculty associates have been involved in discussions and decisions of the university units, they are often able to explain assignments or requests that the university might make of school personnel that would seem on the surface to be imposing or inconsiderate. Because the clinical faculty associates are changed every two years, increasing numbers of teachers in the schools are able to have this inside exposure to and participation in the university culture.

The same partnership has also placed university personnel in boundary-spanning roles. These district liaison directors have a full-time assignment to work with all the partner schools of a designated school district. They consult with the clinical faculty associates about problems involving students, interpersonal and intercultural conflicts, evaluation, and other issues raised by either school or university personnel. These two important groups of partners help to hold diverse parts of the partnership together. The suggestions and encouragement they are able to offer to their colleagues result in better understanding, greater cooperation, and increased patience in many areas that would previously have resulted in conflict.

Realistic Expectations

Educators in the early phases of partnership may begin their collaboration with great expectations for the kinds of renewal that they hope to achieve. Optimism and hope are important qualities for partners to have, but if the hopes are unrealistic, the partners may overextend the agenda or make promises that they will not be able to fulfill. For example, it may not be possible for all stakeholders to be involved, and there are strategies that have been successful in some partnerships that are not readily transferable to others. Needs and resources of partnerships vary, and partnerships with more experience can sometimes carry out plans and projects that would not be possible for beginning collaborators. In addition, some projects or transformations sound better in the conference room than they will be in actual practice. As Goodlad warns, "Fascination with dialogue must never obscure its purpose: the transformation of institutional functions."[39] Partners have to be realistic in their expectations of themselves and each other and focus on changes that are most important in their specific institutions and contexts, rather than attempting to implement every good idea they read about or discuss.

It is also important to keep in perspective the effort and sacrifice behind the gains. Christenson and her associates observe, "We try not to romanticize the process or the outcomes; the costs associated with collaboration are too real and persistent."[40] Realistic expectations are a matter of balancing the needs, context, resources, experiences, and capabilities of each specific partnership.

Sometimes expectations that may have seemed realistic are not realized, and partners need to acknowledge that important gains can be made from adaptations, even in the face of disappointment. In one partnership, teacher educators, university professors in mathematics and science, and schoolteachers on the elementary and high school levels decided to apply for a grant that would provide millions of dollars over several years for the collaborative transformation of mathematics and science programs. They hoped to make a systemic transformation of science and mathematics learning for preservice and inservice teachers, as well as for public school students. Hopes were high, and had the grant been received, there is a good chance that the project would have been successful. But there was strong competition for the grant, and the proposal from this partnership was not fully funded. They received some funding but not enough for the systemic changes that the partners had envisioned. Rather than decide that the efforts and sacrifices of partnership had been wasted, the participants used the money they received to implement some of the important aspects that they had envisioned for the program, including valuable on-site service-learning experiences for teachers and students on all levels, from kindergarten through the doctorate. Bonds were formed among the participants in the initial and revised programs that have lasted many years and have been fruitful in a variety of ways.

Dreaming within a partnership can be exhilarating, and sometimes successes occur that produce feelings of euphoria. Nevertheless, partners need to realize that not all dreams will be completely fulfilled and that euphoria can come from using limited resources in focused and realistic programs, as well as from transforming large areas of university and public school practice.

Appropriate Rewards

In sharing lessons they learned from their experiences in school-university partnerships, Coombs and Hansen acknowledge, "It is easy to say that the program will be mutually beneficial, but it requires continual effort to ensure that it actually is."[41] Providing for some consistency in the area of rewards can be difficult because the reward systems of universities and public school districts differ appreciably, and neither system tends to reward or encourage partnership work.

Sandholtz and Merseth warn that rewards for collaboration and demands of collaboration for public school teachers must be balanced at both the individual and the institutional level;[42] this need for balance is also relevant to university personnel. In addition, the specific rewards must be chosen in accordance with the desires and values of those to be rewarded.

Some universities with strong commitment to teacher education have adapted the faculty reward structure to allow for collaborative projects in and research with the schools to have a place in the advancement and reward system of the institution. Public school participants are sometimes rewarded with adjunct faculty status at the university or with credit toward graduate degrees offered for on-site research and inquiry applied in their classroom. One such institution is designing an entire master's program around classroom inquiry. Such programs and policies are consistent with the comment of Bernard Gifford that existing incentive structures should be altered "to provide rewards specifically for the fruits of collaboration."[43]

Some partnerships reward participating teachers by arranging for them to be released from their regular teaching responsibilities for periods of time so that partnership work will not cut so heavily into their personal time. This is a reward directly related to partnership participation, although it does not reward its products. Sandholtz and Merseth note that "time is the most critical resource for teachers." They cite several studies that document the connection between provision of time for teachers to participate in partnership work and the eventual success of that work.[44] This form of reward does directly affect the sacrifice required, so that teachers are not as likely to withdraw from activity because the sacrifice is burdensome. However, for some teachers, being taken out of their classrooms cuts them off from the reward they value the most: the privilege of working directly with their students. Even when released time is considered a reward by teachers, it may generate difficulties for other partners. Principals may be beset with complaints of parents that giving too many teachers too much released time interferes with classroom continuity and disrupts their children's learning. Brookhart and Loadman summarize the problem and conclude: "When participants in collaboration come with different definitions of what their reward will be, they can end up disagreeing about what it is they should do and why."[45] Thus it is important that partners listen to each other when making decisions on rewards and consider both advantages and hardships that may be incurred by the choice of a particular reward or reward system.

Sandholtz and Merseth caution that rewards that provide support for participation at one stage of the partnership may not suffice over time.[46] Not only does the reward system have to be flexible in fitting the desires and needs of individual participants, it also needs to remain dynamic in order to satisfy individuals whose interests and needs change over time.

Occasions for Sharing

Partnership work provides for rich and varied collaborative experiences, and much is gained when these experiences are shared. In most partnerships, numerous changes, experiments, research developments, and projects are happening at different places; all participants can and should benefit from learning about them. Where comparable challenges are faced in different types of collaborative undertakings, successful and unsuccessful strategies should be discussed. Rosaen and Hoekwater describe a partnership in Michigan that brought school and university personnel together for extended conversations, which included clarifying meanings, sharing interpretations, expressing frustrations, exploring project ideas, examining educational concepts, and proposing changes and new developments. These conversations helped the participants know and relate to one another in a more open, trusting manner, as well as generate ideas for continued collaboration.[47]

Ann Lieberman observed the benefits to the Southern Maine Partnership of providing varied opportunities for partnership members to exchange ideas. Initially, teachers joined in monthly meetings "to discuss research and educational practice." These meetings provided a neutral forum for examining teaching practices and problems in "a safe and nonjudgmental environment." The group was able to discover important commonalities and differences in their experiences. Lieberman found that "as the partnership grew, it also helped to establish a core of committed teachers (as well as superintendents and principals) who were energized by the discussions, by the participants' seriousness of purpose, and by the growing egalitarianism that permeated the group."[48]

Many of the other NNER settings have had experiences similar to those of Southern Maine. They have seen the importance of bringing members together in groups large and small, formal and informal, with membership that spans partnership groupings or membership limited to a specific institution or group, with specified topics or free topic choice. As any partnership expands in participants and projects, the number, types, topics, and purposes of sharing occasions expand as well. Many partnerships have annual conferences or periodic linking conferences. Some partnerships have adapted associates programs modeled on those held by Goodlad and his colleagues in Seattle. Most partnerships hold some form of focused group getaways—called retreats or advances, depending on the sponsoring institution. Lieberman emphasizes the need for variety and flexibility: "A major strength of the [Southern Maine] partnership is its recognition that it must keep changing the kinds of forums it creates to match the growing and deepening needs of its constituents."[49] Regardless of the form and context, the willingness of partners to spend time together deliberating, exploring, listening, and sharing is both an indication of commitment to the relationship and an essential means of creating and clarifying experience.

Conclusion

Building and participating in school-university partnerships is challenging for all participants. It is a little like playing in a jazz band. Jazz musicians bring instruments with different tones and strengths, but they need to have common goals and a common understanding of what they want their performance to be like. They must respect each others' talents and appreciate the contribution that each will be able to make. If they are going to improvise, they must agree on common themes and progressions, with each selecting specific passages on which he or she can make a unique and beneficial contribution. Composed pieces require a different kind of precision, but in any performance situation the players must listen carefully to each other and be willing to make adjustments and adaptations as they go along.

Similarly, participants in school-university partnerships have a variety of functions and capabilities. Underlying all of their activities, projects, research applications, and other endeavors must be mutual respect, coupled with appreciation of each others' talents and contributions. Fundamental themes and goals will guide decisions that are made, as well as adaptations and improvisations that occur. Different functions require different kinds of precision and flexibility, but in all aspects of participation the partners must listen carefully to each other.

Although school-university partnerships have not been documented and analyzed in the past with the thoroughness necessary to inform their current growth, more studies are currently being undertaken. With new studies and developments, those entering into such collaborations will have a broader base of knowledge and experience from which to build.

Centers of pedagogy are natural extensions of the school-university partnership. With an understanding of the challenges involved with school-university partnerships, the elements necessary for effective collaboration, and some of the practical strategies for initiating and maintaining collaboration, prospective partners have a solid foundation on which to build a center of pedagogy.

3

Centers of Pedagogy
The Concept

I n the spring of 1996, one of the authors of this book, as dean of
a college of education, participated on a panel with a group of
presidents and chancellors from several universities to discuss the
renewal of teacher education. One of the chancellors said to him,
"So you have a center of pedagogy. Does the college of education
still play a role in teacher education?"

The dean answered, "Actually, its role is clearer and more critical than ever. The college of education is one of the essential partners in the center of pedagogy."

The chancellor said, "Oh, I'm sorry to hear you say that. I would
think it has little to offer now." His intent, it was subsequently clear,
was to create a center of pedagogy and eliminate the College of Education at his institution.

As the following chapters will illustrate, the presence of a center of pedagogy can not only strengthen the college of education
and the quality of the education of educators, but can also renew
education in the schools through structuring and coordinating the
roles played in school renewal by faculty and administrators in education, in the arts and sciences, and in the public schools.[1] But that
can happen only if all parties are clear about the mission and responsibilities of the center.

A center of pedagogy is a coordinating structure for fostering the
ongoing simultaneous renewal of teacher education and public

schools. It is not "structure" alone that strengthens these functions, but the ways in which this structure promotes shared responsibility of three groups that have seldom been connected previously in any real and systemic sense: faculty in the schools and colleges of education, faculty in the arts and sciences, and faculty in the public schools.

The idea of a teacher education structure that focuses on pedagogy is not new. In 1896, John Dewey called for a department of pedagogy at the University of Chicago to enhance the preparation of teachers, a function that was "being left unduly to the mercy of accident, caprice, routine or useless experiment from lack of scientific training."[2] B. O. Smith, in A Design for a School of Pedagogy, proposed in 1980 that schools of education be reconceptualized into schools of pedagogy. Smith was not arguing for a new entity coexisting with schools of education, but rather for a more effective replacement for schools of education. In fact, he recommended that the word education be dropped because it confuses colleagues in other parts of the university who also are engaged in "education."[3]

Nearly one hundred years after Dewey raised the issue, John Goodlad, who more than anyone else is responsible for generating interest in the concept of a center of pedagogy, made this case:

> A center of pedagogy is both a concept and a setting. As a concept, it brings together simultaneously and integratively the commonly scattered pieces of the teacher education enterprise and embeds them in reflective attention to the art and science of teaching. A center of pedagogy could be named a center of teacher education, of course. But then the concept's implementation might (and probably would) embrace only what the name implies—the conduct of teacher education programs devoid of or apart from inquiry into pedagogy. The common neglect of such inquiry has contributed to the low status of teacher education and, to a considerable degree, of teach-

ing itself. Thus I choose to align with what John Dewey
and B. Othanel Smith were seeking in their stress on
pedagogy. The term *center of pedagogy* connotes for me
an inquiring setting for the education of educators that
embraces schools and universities.[4]

But while it may have its roots in some of the ideas Dewey and
Smith put forth, the center of pedagogy that Goodlad proposed is a
very different concept.

First, a center of pedagogy brings together in no uncertain terms
the *tripartite*—the three key groups involved in the education of educators: faculty in schools and colleges of education, faculty in the
arts and sciences, and faculty in the public schools.[5] It does so simultaneously and integratively. The center of pedagogy brings these
"scattered pieces of the teacher education enterprise" together in a
way that requires that they develop a shared vision of their two important shared responsibilities: for public schools in the United
States and for the education of the teachers who staff them.

Second, a center of pedagogy does not displace any of the members of the tripartite. There are a number of options for where the
center of pedagogy might be located and how it might be governed,
but it should be organized and operated so as to emphasize the
unique qualities that each member brings to an effective program
of ongoing renewal.

Third, the center of pedagogy is an "inquiring setting"; it fosters
inquiry about pedagogy and about learning. Goodlad calls for the
center to give "reflective attention to the art and science of teaching." He further argues that the absence of serious inquiry into pedagogy is in part responsible for the low status of teacher education.
As universities recognize teaching as an important area for inquiry—what some would call research or scholarship—the center
of pedagogy should not only provide support for such research, but
should also be a proponent of formal recognition of inquiry into
pedagogy within the university's system of rewards.

Fourth, the center of pedagogy is not about the education of educators alone, but about the simultaneous renewal of the schools and of the education of educators. As Goodlad has argued, simultaneous renewal is a logical development in American education. Twentieth-century educational reform efforts have invariably focused on either schools or teacher education, and results have not been uniformly satisfactory. The weakness of the separate-reforms approach implies the strength of renewing both simultaneously. "We are not likely to have good schools without a continuing supply of excellent teachers," Goodlad argues. "Nor are we likely to have excellent teachers unless they are immersed in exemplary schools for significant portions of their induction into teaching."[6]

The case studies in subsequent chapters describe two centers that are currently in operation and one that is approaching development. Only one of the three partnerships chose to label the structure a "center of pedagogy." The location of the entity differs for the two existing centers and will probably be completely different when established in the third. At Montclair State University, in Upper Montclair, New Jersey, the unit is called the Center of Pedagogy and is positioned like a three-legged platform floating above the College of Education and Human Services, the arts and sciences faculty, and the schools. One leg rests firmly in each of the three entities. At Brigham Young University, the Center for the Improvement of Teacher Education and Schooling (CITES) is located within the School of Education. At the University of Texas at El Paso, the concept for a center of pedagogy is developing through very strong connections between the El Paso Collaborative and the university, with links being forged between education and the arts and sciences, but it does not yet have a formal name or place. In exploring the generic concept of a center of pedagogy, then, the focus of this chapter is on the essential qualities of centers of pedagogy, whatever they may be called and wherever they might exist; on the enabling conditions and strategies that might bring them into being; and on the outcomes that might be projected from their existence.

Essential Qualities

How can the necessary collaboration among the three entities involved in the education of educators be promoted? As Goodlad suggests, in order to coordinate efforts to improve teacher education and renew schooling, it is necessary "to tighten up this array of loose connections."[7] To complete this tightening, a number of essential qualities need to be developed.

The Tripartite and Shared Vision

Within a center of pedagogy, a shared vision must evolve for the purposes of school and teacher education renewal. A shared vision, Peter Senge explains, is very powerful:

> A shared vision is not an idea. It is not even an important idea such as freedom. It is rather a force in people's hearts, a force of impressive power. It might be inspired by an idea, but once it goes further—if it is compelling enough to acquire the support of more than one person—then it is no longer an abstraction. People begin to see it as if it exists. Few, if any, forces in human affairs are as powerful as a shared vision.[8]

Senge's conclusion that a shared vision becomes a reality when it is held by more than one person understates the complexity of the shared vision known as the center of pedagogy. For a center of pedagogy to advance the simultaneous renewal of teacher education and schools, the vision must be shared by many members of the center's tripartite. Furthermore, shared vision cannot be given by one individual to another—or by a group of individuals to another group—any more than a teacher can give knowledge of a concept to a student or a class directly. All participants must embrace the key ideas of a shared vision so each person is involved in its development and implementation. Of course, as the vision is implemented it will evolve as well.

A center of pedagogy provides opportunities for conversation on important issues pertaining to the continued maintenance and evolution of the shared vision. The shared vision may, in fact, be the most powerful quality of a center of pedagogy: it provides the moral basis for obtaining support and resources needed to carry out the mission; it is the touchstone for the renewal of curriculum in both the schools and the university; it underscores the qualities needed in educators; and it is the focal point for the ongoing inquiry supported by a center.

This is not to suggest that having a shared vision alone will involve the tripartite meaningfully in teacher education or will ensure the safe boundaries and resources that are needed. It is, however, an essential aspect of joining together.

The Critical Role of Inquiry

Inquiry, along with teaching, is at the heart of educational institutions; it is essential to renewal. Goodlad envisions a number of different kinds of inquiry going on simultaneously. First, he advocates inquiry into the purposes of American education—that is, of education in a social and political democracy. This form of inquiry into the schools, colleges, and universities leads to a position on the public purpose of education.[9] A second kind of inquiry must focus on programs needed to prepare educators—and to renew educators already in the schools. Members of the tripartite seek ways to use knowledge from cognitive psychology, human development, sociology, philosophy, and the other disciplines central to understanding teaching and learning in order to forge the best possible programs.[10] Third, there must be inquiry into the effectiveness of the programs offered at each setting.[11] Educators inquire how to know that a program is making a difference, how a program promotes the shared vision, and how to document their efforts and results. Finally, as Goodlad suggests, the conception of scholarship must be broadened to "include more than some people are willing to include under the research umbrella."[12] Educational institutions must engage in and value research about teaching and research about schools.

Ernest Boyer's work *Scholarship Reconsidered: Priorities of the Professoriate* and a later volume, *Scholarship Assessed: Evaluation of the Professoriate*, by Charles Glassick, Mary Taylor Huber, and Gene Maeroff, have helped to broaden the meaning of scholarship, especially in extending it to the scholarship of pedagogy—a focus on teaching—and to the scholarship of application—actual work in schools.[13] Dewey foreshadowed this change by arguing as early as 1904 that schools of education should follow the lead of other professional schools and seize control of their intellectual methods.[14] Applied research is, and has been, valued in such settings.

The current interest in changing conceptions of scholarship goes beyond Dewey in that it recognizes that the redefinition of scholarship is as appropriate for arts and sciences faculty as for education faculty. This redefinition is especially important at universities committed to excellence in teaching and to scholarship related to community service—improving the lives of those in its service area by focusing on persistent social problems. Their adoption of service-learning pedagogies in their courses provides considerable evidence that arts and sciences faculty members share the interest of their education colleagues in social change. Through service-learning, students work off campus in community settings, and their university courses draw on these experiences to explore content issues. Arts and sciences faculty members' interest in changing the roles and reward system is evident in their attendance, along with faculty of medical and law schools, at programs presented annually by the American Association for Higher Education on faculty roles and rewards. This interest should be considered by those developing centers of pedagogy as they define agendas for inquiry that can be shared by education, arts and sciences, and public school faculty.

Some have argued that with the current pressure in higher education to focus on paradigms of learning rather than paradigms of teaching, it is important to define pedagogy to include the study of learning. However, it seems obvious that inquiry into teaching is necessarily linked to inquiry into learning. Successful teaching requires learning, and the act of teaching is not finished until learning occurs. Yet teaching is often evaluated without consideration of whether learning has occurred. Any center of pedagogy has an obligation to maintain the connection between teaching and learning.

Thus, the inquiry promoted by a center of pedagogy must be broadly conceived and include the study of education and educational institutions, of pedagogy that includes both teaching and learning, and of the evaluation of programs. Such inquiry must be seen as the responsibility of all participants; it must contribute to improving the quality of the center's program; and, where possible, it should contribute to the body of knowledge informing the education of educators and the functions of schools.

Partnership for Simultaneous Renewal

Bringing together the tripartite for genuine collaboration, with commitment to a common mission, requires a history of meaningful partnership based on respect, mutual trust, and a belief that partnership is worthwhile for all participants. The recent history of school-university partnerships is well documented.[15] These partnerships have tended to be top-down and dominated by the universities, despite evidence in the literature that this is not an effective relationship.[16] Sirotnik has identified lessons that might be learned from partnership experiences: "dealing with cultural clash," "dealing with schools of education," "sustaining leadership and commitment," "providing adequate resources," "modeling authentic collaboration," "living with goal-free planning, action and evaluation," "avoiding the quick-fix syndrome," "winning the process/substance debate," "avoiding over- and understructuring," and "translating leadership as empowerment and shared responsibility."[17] Some of these lessons are particularly relevant to the three-way partnerships necessary for an effective center of pedagogy.

Cultural similarities and differences. One important lesson is that the partnership must take into account both the different and the shared interests and responsibilities of the parties. Although it is assumed that all three parties have developed a shared interest in the simultaneous renewal of teacher education and public schools, each group has additional interests that are different from those of the others. If centers of pedagogy are conceptualized as the point at which three concentric circles representing education faculty, arts and sciences faculty, and school faculty overlap, some clear territory is defined, but large areas that do not overlap are still the responsibilities of each member group. To be successful, the partnership must build on the shared interests and respect the differences, especially where they conflict. For example, the university needs to place its students with the best possible teachers for their internships, but the schools must work with teachers, in addition to other constituents—school boards and parents, among others—to ensure that this participation enhances learning rather than displaces highly paid and experienced teachers with unpaid and inexperienced interns. This sort of persistent conflict must be made explicit and addressed directly. In addition, faculty and administrators in arts and sciences may feel conflict between their participation in teacher education and their obligation to serve all university students by providing a liberal arts base. Administrators and faculty must be helped to see the connections between working in schools and improving the quality of future university students as part of their overall responsibility to the university community.

Leadership, commitment, and support. Another important lesson is that within a partnership there must be broad agreement on mission and goals relative to the purposes of schooling and teacher education. It is easy to assume that agreement among partnership leaders represents broad agreement among members of the respective organizations, but this is not necessarily the case. The extent to which individuals within the three organizations are drawn into meaningful conversations and agree on important principles increases the extent to which commitment is translated into action. The basis for determining the real level of agreement within the partnership must be on the level of grassroots participation.

Goal-free planning, action, and evaluation. Our argument that effective partnerships need agreement about mission and goals around a shared vision may appear to be in conflict with Sirotnik's admonition to learn to live with goal-free planning, action, and evaluation. He argues that goals become clear only after some action is taken and that living with ambiguity is important in dealing with meaningful issues. This need to learn to live with ambiguity, to forestall closure and avoid "epistemic impulsivity" or the tendency to leap to decisions, is also central to critical-thinking theory. It is one of the qualities Michael Fullan argues for in suggesting the motto "Ready, fire, aim."[18] This does not mean, however, that some short-term goals growing from the shared vision are not needed to guide action. So long as the vision and mission are seen as evolving, closure can be avoided and vitality maintained.

For example, in the development of the Montclair State University Center of Pedagogy, participants agreed early on that the nature of education in a democracy is an important issue; understanding its meaning and implications became a goal to focus discussion. Sustaining discussion around the issue over several years led to deeper levels of agreement about the meaning of democracy, recognition of the conflicts between the public and private purposes of education in a democracy, and the evolution of curricula and programs at the university and in schools to develop qualities important for engaged citizenship. As results, a service-learning strand emerged in teacher education, undertaken by faculty in education and in the arts and sciences; a "school within a school" with a focus on civics and democracy was created in one of the partner schools; and two faculty members in history developed courses in the evolution of American democracy—with particular attention to the implications for schools—for inclusion in general education. The shared vision and mission evolved, becoming deeper and more compelling, and specific actions were taken based on the common beliefs.

Authentic collaboration. A third lesson that should be learned from partnership function is that strong partnerships are built on equity and trust, often leading to a blurring of boundaries and a sharing of power. So long as each member of the tripartite remains in his or her "own world," little risk and little trust are built across the boundaries. Spending time in each other's cultures is a critical dimension of building partnership. For example, university faculty's teaching in the schools and school faculty's sharing university teaching responsibilities are important cross-boundary activities. When lessons occasionally fail and the cloak of invincibility drops, trust can form among the participants. With trust can come meaningful sharing of power, including search committees and curriculum committees formed from all members of the tripartite. These cross-organizational committees, emerging from strong partnerships, would be evidence of a mature center of pedagogy, where responsibility is truly shared.

Shared resources. A fourth lesson from partnership function is that resource issues must be addressed. Partnership requires mutual responsibility for the good of the whole, and mutual responsibility includes sharing resources in some meaningful way—resources in the form of budget, time, equipment, access to libraries and laboratories, and the like.

Equitable rewards. A fifth consideration is that partnerships need to examine the reward structure available to individuals. Sirotnik, in discussing "dealing with schools of education," points to the intractability of schools of education and says, "The primary culprit is a misguided reward system that is an outgrowth of misplaced values, status deprivation, and identity crisis."[19] The concept is also embedded in Goodlad's second postulate, which calls for "rewards for faculty geared to the nature of the field."[20]

In partnerships, rewards are a concern for all participants. It is unlikely that arts and sciences faculty will be sufficiently motivated by the delayed gratification that better future students might represent. There is evidence of a national interest in expanding reward systems among arts and sciences faculty, and this must be addressed as it relates to centers of pedagogy. Establishing rewards for school faculty for their participation in centers of pedagogy is even more difficult, in part because the concept of promotion is tied to leaving teaching in public P–12 schools. Short of changing that concept, which may in fact be a long-term outcome of work in centers of pedagogy, partnerships must be especially conscious of providing school faculty with rewards tied to partnership participation: for example, released time for partnership work or for opportunities to write and publish in collaboration with university colleagues.

There are, then, three essential conditions needed for a center of pedagogy to take root and function. First, a shared vision must exist among the tripartite regarding the purpose of schooling in a democracy, and from that vision a commitment to the simultaneous renewal of teacher education and public schooling must emerge. Second, inquiry must be central to the renewal responsibilities. Such inquiry must be broadly conceived and promoted in order to legitimize scholarship that is applied and that focuses on pedagogy. Third, the interpersonal trust and commitment necessary for the three cultures to merge into one within a center of pedagogy must emerge from partnership participation. The shared vision and mission of such a partnership continue to evolve and be refined through mutual respect for differences and abilities, trust, resource commitment, and attention to rewards.

Enabling Conditions and Persistent Questions

Qualities have been identified that apply to all centers of pedagogy: a shared vision of both the purposes of education in a democracy and the preparation of educators for those settings, a shared responsibility for simultaneous renewal of those areas, a commitment to inquiry as central to the work of a center of pedagogy, and a commitment to collaboration that extends good school-university partnerships to involve faculty from the arts and sciences along with faculty from the college of education and the public schools. Although it is anticipated that every center of pedagogy will embody these qualities, enabling conditions that allow them to be present may differ widely. To assist in examining the case studies in the following chapters, and in anticipation of the establishment of new centers of pedagogy, some persistent questions related to these conditions are identified. Although the answers may differ from one center to another, the questions will be asked in a context of the qualities identified for centers of pedagogy.

Location, Structure, Governance, Responsibility, and Identity

Each center of pedagogy must deal with a number of questions regarding location, structure, governance, responsibility, and identity.

The location and structure of the centers of pedagogy we examine in depth in subsequent chapters differ widely. Many questions are generally asked in making decisions in this area. Should the center be a clearly identified "place"? Should that place be physically outside or within one of the three entities? Should the center be intertwined organizationally with one of the entities? How are the boundaries of the center defined? How can the existing structures that the tripartite occupy be used to support a center of pedagogy through, for example, joint appointment that might cross two or all three entities?

Governance and decision-making procedures must allow for equity and decisiveness in confronting issues. To whom should the center of pedagogy report? How are policies set and carried out? Can leadership for the center come from one of the entities without disfranchising the others? What structures allow for adequate representation of all three entities? How can governance be prevented from becoming so complicated that it stifles creativity?

Responsibility must be clear and unambiguous. How can responsibility that once rested with one of the members of the tripartite now be shared effectively by all three? How can threats to security be dealt with as members from one entity see members from other entities assume work for which members of the first entity were once fully responsible? How can there be assurance that a job will get done when all are responsible?

Having members who identify with a center—who participate in its activities and take responsibility for its mission—is essential to its success. How can membership and participation in the center be provided for all whose presence is necessary? Can membership be at once accessible and meaningful? Can minimum levels of responsibility be set without closing out participants who are needed? Can membership that carries with it responsibility still be attractive? What is the critical mass of membership that is needed? How can there be assurance that the commitment is deep enough from within the entities so that it is not merely the leaders' perception of commitment?

Funding and Budget

One key to the autonomy of an entity is control over its budget. For centers of pedagogy, often carved from three existing structures, this is a difficult but critical condition to meet. If a center starts up with external funding, how can the transition be made to ongoing institutional support? Do the sources of revenue have to be equitable? If one entity is contributing little in the form of resources, will the services of the center still be of value to it? How can the value of the outcomes of the center be shown to contributors? How much security of budget is it reasonable to expect? Is it realistic to expect a center of pedagogy to be any less vulnerable than the entities that form it?

Support from Existing Leadership

Since centers of pedagogy are new entities, often carved out of existing entities, support and understanding from the leadership of existing structures are critical. Do existing leaders—presidents, provosts,

superintendents, deans—see the education of educators and the renewal of schools as important aspects of their responsibility? How
can this belief be nurtured? How can they be persuaded to act on
the belief? What tangible evidence of support is needed?

All of these are difficult but very important questions. In *Teachers for Our Nation's Schools*, after identifying the elements central
to this work, Goodlad comments that "there are many ways to provide for these minimum essentials." However, he also cautions that
"there are many ways to circumvent them while claiming that they
are in place. The only protection against chicanery is the moral
commitment of those in charge."[21] In claiming to have a center of
pedagogy, then, participants must turn to the essential qualities—
qualities that will allow for the important functions to prevail—and
they must be honest in assessing these critical questions that help
define the enabling conditions.

Possible Outcomes

Clearly, establishing a center of pedagogy is difficult, risky work.
One must ask, what can reasonably be expected as outcomes of this
work? First, a center of pedagogy can be expected to unite the tripartite—the faculty in education, faculty in the arts and sciences,
and teaching and administrative faculty in the schools—in accept-
ing as their shared work the simultaneous renewal of teacher education and public schooling.

Second, as participants arrive at a shared vision, the disconti-
nuities that come from disparate views of "what education and
teaching ideally are and what the schools are for" among the tripartite should be reduced, resulting in a cohesive program.[22]

Third, turf issues will be eased by creating neutral turf occupied
by the tripartite on the basis of parity and equity.

Fourth, the knowledge-practice tension that characterizes
school-university partnerships can be minimized by genuine collaboration. This tension is seen in the traditional arguments that

research does not work in the real world or that the practices engaged in by schoolteachers are not cutting edge.[23]

Fifth, what Goodlad hoped for as outcomes of a center of pedagogy can be anticipated:

- An entity "committed solely to advancing the art and science of teaching"

- An entity with its own budget protected from competing interests

- An entity with "authority and responsibility over a student body of specified size and qualities"

- An entity with authority and responsibility over "personnel, materials, equipment, [and] laboratories" needed for the program

- An entity with the faculty, academic and clinical, needed for the program

- An entity in control of admissions

- An entity with access to adequate high-quality field placements for its students[24]

Finally, the ultimate expectation will be better teachers and better schools, with demonstrably better learning for students, the world's future citizens.

Part II

Centers of Pedagogy in Practice

The center of pedagogy is a natural development of the recent national attention to collaboration between universities and public schools. School-university partnerships, networks, or consortia have been effective in generating simultaneous improvement of teacher preparation and of public schools nationwide. But a third partner has received little attention in such groups: the arts and sciences departments of the universities, units that contribute to the subject-area knowledge that teachers must have in order to educate the young. Having not typically been drawn into partnership with teacher education units and schools, these departments have performed what they perceive to be their function in preparing teachers in ways that they perceive to be adequate. Some perform very well; others show little concern and may bury teacher education beneath priorities that they consider more significant within their disciplines. By providing official channels for bringing arts and sciences departments into the networks and partnerships that are devoted to preparing teachers and educating children, the center of pedagogy has the potential to strengthen both the preparation and the education from three dimensions rather than two.

Establishing such a center is not an easy or inexpensive proposition. In addition to sacrificing time, space, funding, and personnel, all three groups must be willing to sacrifice tradition, turf, and control and to swallow their pride. Administrative formalities seem prohibitive, interpersonal conflicts are likely, and external funding must usually be obtained. But there are universities that have overcome some barriers and established centers of pedagogy that are making significant strides in bringing the three partners together into a focused, unified teacher preparation and school renewal effort. The results have been exciting.

The following three chapters describe the development of two functioning centers of pedagogy and one that might be termed a "center in process." All are at different stages of growth and function. Although the settings are different and many of the circumstances and events that have influenced the development of and concepts behind the centers are unique to those settings, they nevertheless share a number of characteristics.

The three have been included because of their surface diversity and underlying similarities. Teacher education at all three institutions has had times of positive growth and development along with times of discouragement and devaluation. The turning point upward for all three has been the point at which teacher educators have reached beyond the confines of their own offices and classrooms to join with school administrators and teachers to focus on what will best serve the coming generation of teachers and children. As the expanded groups of colleagues have shared their vision, their goals, and their resources, progress has been made toward better teachers and better schools.

Two of the universities—Montclair State University in New Jersey and Brigham Young University in Utah—have now expanded the collegial group to bring in the arts and sciences partners. Important collaborative projects as well as new administrative structures and functions have been established. The third institution, the University of Texas at El Paso, is enjoying the benefits of partnership through a network with school districts and community leaders and is experimenting with ways of involving cross-campus faculty as well. Although official channels and structures have not been established, university leaders have learned through their membership in the National Network for Educational Renewal and association with participants at Montclair and Brigham Young of the potential functions and benefits of the centers. They are looking toward establishing such a center, but one does not yet exist there.

All three case studies begin by describing the university setting and looking at the historical role of teacher education at the institution. All three institutions have been renewed and transformed by the development of collaborative relationships. The case studies of Montclair State and Brigham Young universities describe the development of each center of pedagogy and then explain aspects of the function and some of the achievements associated with the center. The El Paso case study describes collaborative activities and accomplishments that are leading the institution in the direction of a center.

The similarities are widespread; most issues and developments can be easily generalized to a variety of institutions. Even the differences, however, should help to validate our claim that regardless of circumstantial variation, the needs of preservice teachers and schoolchildren can be most effectively addressed through the use of collaborative structures.

4

Montclair State University, New Jersey

In November 1995, after four years of planning, Montclair State University's Center of Pedagogy opened. Its "Rationale and Description," published by the university, describes the Center of Pedagogy as a "place where the education of educators is conceptualized, planned for, and carried out. Its members," the document continues, "include all those committed to, and whose participation is necessary for, that endeavor. Its goal is the facilitation of the ongoing simultaneous renewal of the education of educators, the educational program of the university, and the educational program of the schools in the interest of student learning."[1] The key to the unique function and effectiveness of the Center of Pedagogy is the phrase "all those committed to, and whose participation is necessary for, that endeavor."

For many years, individuals whose work was necessary for the effectiveness of teacher education were scattered through many colleges and departments of the university. Although many were highly committed to the preparation of teachers, often their work was less efficient and less effective than it might have been because it was isolated from the work of those in the College of Education and Human Services and from the work of educators in the public schools. Finally in the Center of Pedagogy, all participants would be able to work together with maximum efficiency and collegiality. The first director of the Center, hired through a national search, held faculty rank in one of the departments of the College of Education and Human Services; however, she could just as readily have come from one of the departments of the arts and sciences or from one of the member districts of the New Jersey Network for Educational Renewal (NJNER). At the Center of Pedagogy these three groups are equal in status and consideration.

The development of the Center of Pedagogy at Montclair State represents the dedicated efforts and the personal and professional sacrifices of a number of stakeholders in the preparation of teachers and the renewal of public schools. Many aspects of its history are unique to the Montclair State setting; others are common to teacher preparation institutions throughout the United States. This case study demonstrates how both individual and common factors have interacted as the Center has evolved.

Development of the Center of Pedagogy

Although the Center of Pedagogy at Montclair State has been in operation only since 1995, its most important underlying factor, a vision of teacher education and school renewal shared by various groups that contribute to these operations, has evolved over a considerably longer period of time. To understand the establishment, operation, and effectiveness of the Center, it is necessary to examine some of the ups and downs associated with this development.

The Setting

Any administrative structure is the product of and must be responsive to the setting in which it functions. The processes involved in the development of the Center are products of both the strengths and the challenges of the Montclair State context.

Montclair State University, with a student body of sixty-five hundred full-time undergraduates, thirty-five hundred part-time undergraduates, and some thirty-five hundred graduate students, is located in northern New Jersey, fifteen miles west of Manhattan. It is part of New Jersey's state college-university system.[2] Montclair is a multipurpose regional university, with five schools and colleges: the College of Education and Human Services, the College of Humanities and Social Sciences, the College of Science and Mathematics, the School of the Arts, and the School of Business. The full-time faculty of 440 and a cadre of adjunct faculty are represented by a local unit of the American Federation of Teachers (AFT). The statewide AFT Council negotiates salary and broad contract issues across all campuses of the state college and university sector, while the local union and administration negotiate such matters as procedures for promotion, for joint appointments, and for doctoral faculty appointments. The local contract is more detailed than the state contract and covers many issues critical to teacher education.

The College of Education and Human Services contains six departments. Four of these are directly involved in teacher education: Curriculum and Teaching; Educational Foundations; Counseling, Human Development and Educational Leadership; and Reading and Educational Media. The others—Human Ecology and Health, and Physical Education, Recreation and Leisure Studies—include programs to prepare teachers but have other responsibilities as well. The college has eighty full-time faculty and is governed through a faculty senate and an administrative council consisting of chairs, the dean, and an assistant dean.

The New Jersey Network for Educational Renewal is a school-university partnership consisting of Montclair State University and twenty school districts that have partner schools or professional development schools working in collaboration with the university.[3] Most of its funding comes from the university, but member districts pay dues, the amount depending on the size of the district. There is a full-time director, who holds faculty rank in the College of Education and Human Services. The NJNER is governed through an executive committee chaired by the NJNER director and consisting of the director of the Center of Pedagogy, the dean of the College of Education and Human Services, and representatives from each district. An operations committee, which includes coordinators from each district, plans the NJNER activities, such as ongoing professional development activities and summer programs. Through the NJNER, school faculty become clinical faculty of the university and members of the Center of Pedagogy.

Evolution of the Setting and Its Mission

Like many other state universities, Montclair State University began as a normal school. At times during its development, the function of preparing teachers has been central to its purpose and functions. But at other times the growth of additional programs and departments has obscured and on occasion seemed to discredit the teacher education work, a sequence not unusual among normal schools that have developed into universities with more varied offerings.

Founding and Early Development

The New Jersey Normal School at Montclair was founded in 1908 as New Jersey's second normal school for the training of elementary teachers. Its first executive officer was a principal, not a president. In 1926, a study found that nearly 90 percent of the state's secondary teachers were trained outside New Jersey. Since there were five normal schools for elementary teachers and a fifth about to be constructed, it was decided in 1927 that Montclair should become the state's first teachers college, with a mission to prepare junior and senior high school teachers.[4]

When the institution became Montclair State Teachers College in 1927, students selected a subject-area major and minor; they did not major in education. In 1932 Montclair became the first of the original six normal schools to offer a master's degree. The college received accreditation by the Middle States Association of Colleges and Schools in 1937, in accordance with liberal arts standards, although it was still a teachers college; it was the first in the nation, other than Teachers College at Columbia University, to be so accredited.

In 1958, Montclair State Teachers College merged with the Panzer College of Physical Education and Hygiene to become Montclair State College. All graduating students continued to be certified to teach until 1966, when the college was recognized as a comprehensive college and began to offer nonteaching liberal arts programs. In 1994, it was the first of the six former state normal schools to be designated a university by the state.

The Dark Ages

John Goodlad calls attention to a phenomenon that has often occurred with evolving normal schools and teachers colleges: "The transition from normal school to regional state university and from teaching to research together appear to have contributed significantly to the insecure status of teacher education and faculty members connected with it." The transition, he continues, leads to "a decline in status of the unit labeled 'Education' and a corresponding decline in status for teacher education."[5] For Montclair State University, that critical point when status was diminished for teacher education seems to have come in 1966, eight years after the name was changed from Montclair State Teachers College to Montclair State College, the point at which students were no longer required to seek teacher certification as part of their programs.[6] As long as all students were seeking certification, all of the faculty were teacher educators. Many liberal arts faculty who left for summer break in May 1966 as teacher educators returned that September reborn as "purists" in their disciplines. They began to distance themselves from teacher education. Some have described the period from 1966 until the early 1980s as the "dark ages for teacher education."[7]

Numerous anecdotes can illustrate this distancing. For example, when a high-ranking college-level administrator who had been a faculty member in philosophy of education left his administrative position to return to the faculty, he chose to return to the newly formed Department of Philosophy and to have nothing more to do with educational philosophy. During this period, the faculty in education had virtually no control over the curriculum that prepared teachers. When the faculty was preparing for a National Council for Accreditation of Teacher Education (NCATE) review in the 1970s, it was clear that the curriculum had to be changed to add a course in the foundations of education, then an NCATE requirement. The dean of the School of Education made a plea for this course to the College Curriculum Committee, which had to approve even the most minute change in all programs. The committee refused, and he stormed out in anger. The vice president for academic affairs promised to consider the course despite the actions of the committee. In a meeting with the dean, the president, and several administrators in the School of Education, the vice president for academic affairs announced that he had reconsidered and would approve the course, but only if something else in teacher education was cut.

The lack of control and the lack of any sense of self-governance in the School of Education, along with the disrespect of the larger university for anything connected with teacher education, was palpable. Ultimately, it took a conditional accreditation decision from NCATE for the course in foundations to be approved. But the course remains in the curriculum today, and Montclair State is one of the few institutions of its kind with a strong, independent Department of Educational Foundations.

Renaissance

By the late 1970s, after teacher education had endured more than a decade of neglect, several initiatives undertaken by the teacher education faculty began to attract the attention of a new university president and then a new vice president for academic affairs. These initiatives centered on work with urban schools and on critical thinking. One of the first large-scale staff development projects focusing on critical thinking was Project THISTLE: Thinking Skills in Teaching and Learning. The project was first funded in 1979 and has continued to attract foundation support through 1998. Its target was the Newark public schools. A second involvement, with the fledgling Newark Teachers Center, marked the beginning of a long-term commitment to urban education.

In 1980, the college was reorganized and the School of Professional Studies was created, bringing together the departments in the former School of Education and Community Services and those of another unit, the School of Professional Arts and Sciences. The reorganization was actually undertaken to create a separate School of Business that could achieve accreditation. A new dean of the School of Professional Studies was selected, an internal candidate whose background was in teacher education. Although the work in the Newark Center continued, the new dean focused much of his attention on the departments in the new School of Professional Studies with programs other than teacher education—the Departments of Home Economics, Recreation, Physical Education, Health, and Industrial Studies—in order to establish credibility with a new constituency.[8]

In the early 1980s an opportunity to focus on teacher education arose when the director of student teaching retired and the Office of Teacher Education was established. A faculty member with a strong commitment to and roots in teacher education was appointed director of teacher education,[9] and his office slowly assumed more responsibility for programmatic issues of teacher education in addition to its former administrative functions. This change was not without controversy. Some faculty felt that the title "director of teacher education" should be "director of the office of teacher education," a subtle but significant difference.

The issue of the title faded when a more significant challenge to teacher education appeared on the scene in 1981. The governor, along with his commissioner of education, announced the New Jersey Alternate Route Program, a form of certification designed to allow school districts to hire liberal arts graduates with minimal preparation in education as certified teachers. Teacher educators in

New Jersey opposed the proposal, which they viewed as a threat to their very existence. For some colleges, including Montclair State, the Alternate Route was a catalyst that forced much closer collaboration with constituent school systems. The dean, the director of teacher education, and the superintendent of the Montclair public schools presented testimony on the Alternate Route to the New Jersey State Board of Education, proposing that a consortium of schools and colleges work together to provide a program leading to certification. This proposal foreshadowed the subsequent networks of school-university collaboration that culminated in the New Jersey Network for Educational Renewal; it even included reference to future professional development schools.

Another outcome of the Alternate Route experience was the beginning of engagement by the School of Professional Studies in state and national education politics and policymaking. The dean had attended meetings of the New Jersey Association of Colleges for Teacher Education (NJACTE)—the state's affiliate of the American Association of Colleges for Teacher Education (AACTE)—when he was a department chair. NJACTE assumed leadership against the Alternate Route and secured the help of members of the national staff of AACTE, as well as financial support from the national association. This introduction to AACTE became important in the evolution of teacher education at Montclair State University.

Evolution of a Point of View and a Shared Vision

Perhaps the most significant development in teacher education at Montclair State has been the evolution of a shared vision about teaching, teacher education, and schools. This vision began with collaborative efforts to promote critical thinking in Newark schools and was gradually refined and expanded to include a diversity of individuals and organizations involved in all aspects of public school and teacher education renewal.

The institution began its significant work in teaching for critical thinking with the Institute for the Advancement of Philosophy for Children and its influential, philosophy-based critical-thinking curriculum for children, now adopted in more than seventy nations.[10] Later, Project THISTLE extended the conception of critical thinking originally developed in that institute to all areas of school curriculum using existing school texts and materials. By 1986 the work on critical thinking developed to the point that a group of faculty, working with the dean and the director of teacher education, began to conceptualize the entire teacher education program around the theme of critical thinking. The theme was infused throughout the curriculum. Subsequently, Montclair State established the Institute for Critical Thinking as an arm of the provost's office to provide leadership for the infusion of critical thinking throughout the curriculum of the college. Thus, critical thinking, the theme of the teacher education program, became more broadly based and began to emerge in liberal arts programs, in other professional programs, and eventually throughout the college and the university.

In order to ensure that a core of teachers and schools understood the theme of the program, the Clinical Schools Network was established in 1986. Inspired by the National Network for Educational Renewal (NNER), it was subsequently reorganized as the New Jersey Network for Educational Renewal.

In 1991 the dean of the School of Professional Studies became aware of John Goodlad's call for teacher education programs to join in a national renewal effort.[11] The dean received the application for membership in the NNER and sent it to the director of teacher education along with a note saying, "With establishing the new Professional Development School in Newark and the expansion of our network, I'm not sure we have time to develop a response to this application and get involved. What do you think?" The director responded, "I'll prepare a draft for you to consider."

The draft was about fifty pages long. A site visit followed, and Montclair State and the NJNER together became one of eight settings in the NNER. Montclair State received a planning grant of $25,000, matched by the New Jersey Department of Higher

Education and the university, to begin renewal. Affiliation with the NNER has been a defining event in the evolution of Montclair State University.

The most important aspect of the renewal process was the refinement and extension of the shared vision of the teacher education program. Through discussions and retreats (Montclair calls them "advances"), stakeholders in the program developed the mission around the framework of critical thinking, access to knowledge, nurturing pedagogy, stewardship of best practice, and enculturation into a political and social democracy.[12] The moral dimensions of each became increasingly important. A clear statement of expectations for students, the "Portrait of a Teacher," emerged as a framework for recruitment, admission, curricular planning, certification decisions, and professional development.[13]

In 1994, Montclair State College became Montclair State University by action of the Department of Higher Education. Later that year, the School of Professional Studies became the College of Education and Human Services. In November 1995 the nation's first Center of Pedagogy began operation.

Essential Qualities of a Center of Pedagogy

Reflection on the development and first years of operation of the Center of Pedagogy has shown that there are certain qualities and relationships that must be present for a Center of Pedagogy to function to its fullest capacity. Although not tangible or easy to define or assess, these characteristics are important in making feasible the establishment and operation of this kind of collaborative structure.

A Shared Vision Across the Tripartite

Much has been done to promote a shared vision at Montclair State University and its partner schools. One of the first aspects to be shared was the focus on critical thinking between 1979 and 1986, when critical thinking was widely infused as a theme throughout the program for teacher education, and subsequently throughout the university. Since 1987, workshops and programs, including summer institutes, have been held by the Institute for Critical Thinking, as well as the Clinical Schools Network and its successor, the NJNER.

Beginning in 1990, a number of January advances were held for university and school faculty and selected students in teacher education, typically over three days in January, a time when most faculty could participate. At these advances, twenty-five to thirty faculty members from education, the arts and sciences, and the schools met to discuss issues related to the program, with a focus on critical thinking in the early years, broadened in the later years to include the dimensions of teaching suggested by Goodlad's work. These additional dimensions included infusing democracy into the curriculum, exploring the meaning of access to knowledge, and examining the moral dimensions of all aspects of the program. The meetings sometimes gave rise to discussion groups that continued throughout the year, and they often led to personal commitments by participating faculty. For example, after an advance that focused on the role of the school in democracy, all participants were asked to answer questions concerning their personal commitment to enhance their knowledge of democracy and to consider how it could be reflected in both the preparation of educators and the mission and curricula of P–12 schools. The questions led to the formation of a study group that worked throughout the year and brought conclusions and suggestions to the next advance, creating continuity.

One of the most significant vehicles for creating a shared vision has been the Leadership Associates Program. Beginning in 1993, the Institute for Educational Inquiry invited the university–public school networks affiliated with the NNER to nominate faculty and administrators to serve as Leadership Associates. These individuals spent four weeks during the year studying in Seattle with a core of faculty and reading texts relevant to the Agenda for Education in a Democracy. Montclair has had a participant in each of the Seattle leadership programs, with representatives coming from education, the arts and sciences, and the schools. This core of leaders in turn developed a local leadership associates program at the university, through which twenty faculty members a year—from the schools, the education faculty, and the arts and sciences faculty—complete a two-week summer program of reading, discussion, and study, with attendance at all meetings a requirement. Each cohort meets again several times during the year and reconvenes in the summer to discuss progress. All participants must undertake an inquiry project, original research designed to advance the work of teacher education and public school renewal. Through an inquiry project, an individual or group of individuals identifies a problem in the ongoing renewal process and seeks solutions for it. Examples of such projects include establishing a civics and government school-within-a-school at a high school; developing ways to promote democratic practices; equipping beginning teachers to use culturally responsive teaching to be more effective with language minority and immigrant students; and enhancing consistency between the university's admissions practices and its curriculum. By 1998 more than eighty participants had completed the program. These individuals, many of them recruited because they are opinion leaders in their own areas, have a responsibility to involve others they work with in the renewal effort. They have all become members of the Center of Pedagogy and now constitute the leadership core of the work. The leadership associates program was originally funded through external grants, but it is now funded as part of the university's budget.[14]

Focus on Inquiry

Inquiry into pedagogy, the education of educators, and the purposes of schools among the faculty in education, the arts and sciences, and the public schools evolved as a central activity at the university and took many forms. Among these were the establishment of teacher study groups in partner schools and at the university, the evolution of renewal grants to support more sustained study and change in settings, and inquiry projects growing out of a local leadership associates program.

Meaningful Partnership for Sustained Simultaneous Renewal

It became obvious when the theme of critical thinking was infused throughout the teacher education program that P–12 schools must be staffed with faculty who understood the theme to provide logical placement sites for students. Critical thinking as a basis for education was not widely understood in the schools. The roles of teachers and administrators in the schools would need to be expanded if the critical-thinking focus was to be a success.

Development of the Clinical Schools Network

This necessity gave birth to the university-school partnership called the Clinical Schools Network and subsequently known as the New Jersey Network for Educational Renewal. It began with the focus of sponsoring professional development for teachers who would become cooperating teachers or clinical faculty. The director of teacher education, with the help of a retired superintendent, managed the NJNER and sought to train prospective cooperating teachers and develop field sites from it.

In its first years, the NJNER conducted ongoing professional development for faculty, primarily through a summer institute. The university supported this work through the Institute for Critical Thinking and provided a stipend for teacher participants and program faculty. From the beginning, university and school faculty shared the responsibility for presenting workshops about critical thinking.

Over time, with the maturation of the shared vision, the nature of the NJNER became more complex and formal. Early on, it adopted a mission statement that reflected the emerging shared vision of the program for educators, a statement that continues to govern the NJNER:

> The New Jersey Network for Educational Renewal promotes the simultaneous renewal of the schools and the

education of educators through a collaboration between
and among Montclair State University and member
school districts as equal partners. The Network seeks to
balance self-interest and selflessness in the provision of
teacher preparation, professional development, curricular development and research. Through an emphasis on
critical thinking, the Network strives to provide the best
possible education for all students, enabling them to
make good judgments and to become contributing citizens in a political and social democracy.[15]

Criteria for membership in the NJNER include agreeing to participate actively in its mission and work and its governance for at
least two years, selecting a district coordinator, and consenting to
give preference to Montclair State University students for field experiences. In turn, the university agrees to provide a director, space,
support staff, and materials for the work of the NJNER. In addition,
the university provides space and funding for the professional development programs, connects university faculty with school needs,
facilitates grant writing and manages grants, and engages in evaluation of the work.[16]

The NJNER has gone beyond its initial purpose of recruiting
clinical adjunct faculty to work in the teacher education program
and provide reinforcing placement for students. In its expanded goal
of promoting simultaneous renewal in the schools as the program
for teacher education is renewed, it has developed a number of de-
vices, including the establishment of teacher study groups and renewal grants within the schools.

Expansion of Clinical Faculty Roles

In addition to serving as clinical supervisors for students in the
teacher education program, the clinical faculty of the schools sometimes assume traditional roles of university faculty: functioning as
university supervisors; teaching courses in the professional sequence,
either alone or teamed with a university faculty member; even in-

structing graduate courses. Frequently they work with teachers in their own or other districts in professional development work, exemplifying the philosophy of the NJNER that the university is not the only source of expertise and ideas for renewal. Cross-district professional development is encouraged. Finally, clinical faculty have written articles with university faculty, have participated with them in national meetings of the American Association of Colleges for Teacher Education and the Holmes Group, and have been involved on NCATE committees that are redesigning standards. These expanded roles are encouraged by the districts, and faculty from the schools frequently report on the impact of their broader professional involvement on their own sense of worth and status within the district. All clinical faculty members from NJNER schools are members of the Center of Pedagogy.

Professional Development Schools

Naturally, it is not possible for the university to work directly with all schools in all districts, which range from small suburban districts to the largest urban districts in the state, including the Newark and Paterson public schools. Instead, partner schools within each district are identified initially as focal points for recruiting clinical faculty and promoting professional development work. A school is invited to become a professional development school when it exhibits a high level of commitment to the Agenda for Education in a Democracy, including a willingness to examine curriculum and mission; when the school district superintendent and board commit to the collaboration; and when resources exist to assign at least one university faculty member to the institution one-quarter time through the Faculty Scholarship Incentive Program. To date, four schools have become professional development schools.

Mission and Functions of the Center of Pedagogy

The Center of Pedagogy at Montclair State University opened officially in November 1995. The Center was placed in a building occupied by offices associated with the College of Education and Human Services, but outside the main administrative offices of the college. In effect, the Center is envisioned as an entity floating outside its three partner participants: the College of Education and Human Services, the other colleges and schools of the university, and the school districts represented in the NJNER.

The implications of this conception are reflected in the Center's mission and function, staffing, governance, and membership. They bear on the discussions of joint appointments, and on the authority for curricular decisions. They are illustrated by the dual reporting responsibility of the director of the Center. However, symbolically and in reality, the responsibility for teacher education rests with the Center, with each constituent part contributing its unique expertise.

Mission of the Center of Pedagogy

The Center of Pedagogy is "a place where the education of educators is conceptualized, planned for, and carried out." One of the first tasks of the Center's advisory board was to adopt a mission statement:

> The mission of the Center of Pedagogy is the continuing development of educators who promote students' critical thinking and learning and develop their competence to participate actively and productively in democratic communities. The Center's members recognize their roles and moral responsibilities in the enculturation of students into our emerging political and social democracy. The Center provides a vehicle for collaboration in an environment where all members can participate as equals. The Center of Pedagogy facilitates the ongoing simultaneous renewal of the education of educators and the educational programs of the university and the public schools. The Center encourages a wide range of scholarship, especially the scholarship of pedagogy and of application. The Center of Pedagogy is char-

acterized by shared governance and open communication involving all interested parties.[17]

All of the important functions of the Center are identified between the definition and the mission statement. The Center is responsible for conceptualizing, planning, and carrying out teacher education through its various offices. It maintains the moral commitment to the mission of enculturation into a political and social democracy and to access to knowledge. The Center is the vehicle for collaboration among faculty in education, faculty in the schools, and faculty in the arts and sciences, and it is responsible for coordinating their efforts in the ongoing simultaneous renewal of the education of educators and the work of schools. The Center encourages scholarship and thus becomes, as Goodlad suggested, "an inquiring setting for the education of educators that embraces schools and universities."[18]

The Inquiry Functions

The Center carries out all of the critical inquiry functions Goodlad identified: inquiry into the needs and characteristics of schools, the preparation programs of educators, and teaching. Much of this work is done jointly between university faculty and school faculty through the NJNER, which has taken a number of steps to ensure this ongoing inquiry.

First, teacher study groups were established. Partner school educators were asked to propose inquiry projects to be undertaken by groups of teachers to promote the shared mission of the NJNER and the schools. A small amount of money, usually $500, was provided for each study group to pay for books, refreshments, and the like. An extraordinarily wide range of areas of study emerged, all related to the mission and designed to promote renewal.

Second, through a DeWitt Wallace–Reader's Digest Fund Incentive Award in Teacher Education administered by the Institute for Educational Inquiry in Seattle, which was matched by the university and by outside sources, the NJNER made renewal grants of $5,000 available to the partner schools. These grants were used for broader undertakings than the study groups but were similarly designed to promote renewal and to require involvement of university faculty.

Third, the NJNER secured an additional grant from a local foundation known for its support of education in order to make larger renewal grants available to four schools. This foundation had not previously worked through a university for this sort of work; thus, the project is an important example on which to build for the future.

In addition, the university's Faculty Scholarship Incentive Program (FSIP) has supported ongoing research by university faculty in and about school settings. This research, which focuses on scholarship of pedagogy and of application, has yielded articles, books, and national conference presentations to advance understanding of teaching and learning.

Finally, with support from the National Education Association (NEA) and the university, two university faculty with public school faculty partners are engaging in ongoing documentation, evaluation, and analysis of the simultaneous renewal efforts.

Leadership and Staffing Components

Conceptually, the position of director of the Center of Pedagogy could have been tied to faculty rank in the College of Education and Human Services, to faculty rank in the other colleges and schools of the university, or to a position in the public school system; however, to simplify matters, the first search specified faculty rank in one of the departments of the College of Education and Human Services, but without specifying the department.

The search committee, chaired by a faculty member from the College of Education and Human Services, included members from education, the arts and sciences, and the schools in approximately equal numbers. A national search yielded the first director. Although the faculty appointment could have been made in Counseling and Administration or Curriculum and Teaching, it was placed in Counseling. A good deal of the early work of the Center was expected to focus on the elements of the teacher education program housed in Curriculum and Teaching, so it was felt that placing the director's line in Curriculum and Teaching might restrict her freedom to act independently of that department. A later search for the second director of the Center included the possibility of a joint appointment between two academic departments or between an academic department and the Center, an option not open at the time of the first search. Development of a mechanism for joint appointments was the last of the critical components of the Center of Pedagogy to become complete. Because of lengthy negotiations with the union, the issue was not settled until spring 1997, more than a year and a half after the Center had opened.

To carry out the Center's functions, the director, with the help of members of the advisory board, uses negotiation and authority. For example, in establishing nine task forces with very specific charges to recommend changes for the ongoing renewal of the education of educators, the director cut across the three member groups. These task forces undertook discussion, research, and policy recommendations around such issues as a five-year program, recruitment and retention of minority candidates, the professional sequence, general education, and the renewal of the program for school administrators. The director met with each department in the College of Education and Human Services and the College of Humanities and Social Sciences to discuss the Center's role and the colleges' role in the programs. The director cosigns certificates of completion of the leadership associates program, along with the coordinator of the Agenda for Education in a Democracy. The director also has final authority to resolve individual problems students have with admissions, program completion, placement, and the like.

The complex job of director is facilitated by a strong support staff of three full-time professional staff members, four university faculty with almost full-time commitment to the Center, three secretaries, and four graduate assistants. The director's time is devoted almost entirely to providing leadership. (The teaching responsibility is one course per year.) Additional support comes from faculty on FSIP who devote their time to work in schools.

The director began the assignment in July 1995 by conducting a session with the university's first leadership associates group around the definition of a center of pedagogy. A series of meetings followed with staff from offices that were to be incorporated into the Center beginning in September:

- The Office of Teacher Education and Placement, under the direction of a former assistant superintendent of schools, is responsible for the orientation of university and school supervisors and for the placement of students for fieldwork and for their first professional positions.

- The Office of Admissions, directed by a professional staff person and a secretary, coordinates admission and retention for all students in teacher education.

- The Curriculum Resource Center, under the direction of a professional staff person and several graduate assistants, is a curriculum library and resource center that focuses on the use of technology in education.

- The office of the NJNER, directed by a faculty member with a part-time secretary and a graduate assistant, coordinates the work of the NJNER.

- The office of the Agenda for Education in a Democracy, under the direction of a faculty member with a part-time secretary and a graduate assistant, tracks the renewal work and manages grants related to that work.

- The National Education Association/Teacher Education Initiative office, staffed by two faculty members with a graduate assistant and part-time secretary, works with the NEA in implementing the teacher education initiative. It manages the overall evaluation of the renewal of teacher education, coordinates relationships with the professional associations in the schools, and establishes professional development schools.

- Project THISTLE: Teaching Skills in Teaching and Learning, directed by a faculty member and a graduate assistant, manages the staff development program around critical thinking in the Newark public schools.

- The Teacher Education Advocacy Center, directed by one faculty member with two professional staff persons and a graduate assistant, recruits, counsels, and supports students from underrepresented groups.

All but two of these offices are located on the first floor of the university building housing the major portion of the College of Education and Human Services. The budget and the responsibility for supervising the individuals in these offices were transferred from the College of Education and Human Services to the Center of Pedagogy in September 1995. Where individuals in these offices also hold a faculty rank, the director and the dean share responsibility for supervising each participant's work.

All of the administrative and support structures relating to teacher education have been placed under the auspices of the Center of Pedagogy.

Governance

To whom should the Center of Pedagogy report? How should policies be set and carried out? These were not simple questions. The answers are not simple either, and probably will be different in every setting that has a center of pedagogy.

At Montclair, the thought of aligning the Center of Pedagogy with the provost's office was considered but rejected, since the provost does not have any authority over the public schools, which represent one-third of the tripartite membership of the Center.

Reporting to the provost would, it was decided, disfranchise this important constituency. The Center's reporting entirely to the dean of the College of Education and Human Services was rejected as well, since that would disfranchise two constituencies: the schools and the arts and sciences faculty.

Instead, an advisory board of the Center was appointed to include faculty from education, the arts and sciences, and the schools, as well as administrators from the schools, the dean of the College of Education and Human Services, and the dean of the College of Science and Mathematics. This board, which meets at least quarterly, establishes policy and oversees the operation of the Center. It is to the advisory board that the director reports in the role of director. In the faculty role, the director is evaluated by an academic department and a dean.

In its first year, the advisory board, whose chair rotates among the tripartite with each meeting, established policy for membership, launched nine task forces to review aspects of teacher education, and met with chairs and members of each task force to hear their recommendations. In conducting its work, the board held two all-day retreats and three other afternoon or evening meetings.

Another entity now within the Center of Pedagogy and chaired by the director is the Teacher Education Policy Committee. This university senate committee, with members from each tripartite group, is responsible for recommending any changes in university policy and curriculum for teacher education. When a teacher education curriculum matter is recommended through the departmental structure, it does not go to the university's Curriculum Committee. Instead, the Teacher Education Policy Committee serves as the curriculum committee for all matters concerning teacher education.

Membership

Earlier, a definition given for the Center of Pedagogy stated that the "members of the Center of Pedagogy include all those committed to, and whose participation is necessary for" the conceptualization of, planning for, and carrying out of the education of educators. This is the goal toward which a center of pedagogy must continue to work as it seeks to have all necessary participants hold membership.

The advisory board of the Center struggled with the question of membership. It was important to be inclusive, to have membership stand for something, and to have it be attractive. Since members continue to hold status in their home departments, schools, or colleges, membership in the Center had to be structured so that it did not interfere with any other memberships.

First, it was decided that all NJNER clinical faculty members would be members of the Center. Supervisors, principals, and superintendents could become members of the Center by becoming clinical faculty. Second, university members were invited to complete an application process and to attend an orientation meeting to attain membership. Faculty could reach another level of membership by seeking a joint appointment between an academic department and the Center of Pedagogy. Third, leadership associates would be members constituting the Leadership Council of the Center, advising the director on expanding membership, along with other important issues.

All individual members receive a certificate of membership and must maintain membership by attending at least one Center of Pedagogy activity each year. Institutional membership is open to professional associations, businesses, and corporations that make a commitment to the mission of the Center and pay institutional dues. All NJNER member school districts are institutional members of the Center of Pedagogy.[19] In addition, all members of the advisory board hold Center of Pedagogy membership during their term of office.

Honorary membership is granted by the Center of Pedagogy Advisory Board; the first honorary members were John I. Goodlad and the president and provost of the university.

Membership for some is symbolic, representing a commitment to teacher education as conceptualized at Montclair State University and the NJNER. Keeping membership simple and open has avoided a sense of elitism, and care has been taken to ensure that membership does not conflict with other responsibilities and memberships that participants may have. The variation of involvement of members is, of course, significant. The goal, however, is to have as many committed members as possible.

Budget

It is always important to understand the cost of innovations, since finances often become barriers to change. In one typical fiscal year, the university's base allocation to the Center of Pedagogy was $607,000. In addition, the salaries of faculty in the College of Education and Human Services who have almost full-time responsibilities in the Center came to $185,000. The total annual cost therefore was $792,000. Of the base operating costs—the $607,000—about $150,000 was new funding from the university, and the balance was funding of teacher education operations previously included in the College of Education and Human Services.

In addition, the Center had, for the same fiscal year, about $300,000 in external funding, which included grants, contracts, and dues generated by member districts of the NJNER. Some of the funding—the funding from NEA, for example—provided support for important evaluation work. Much of the funding went to support the work of the NJNER. It could be argued that the Center also had the support of the proportion of faculty salaries dedicated to FSIP projects working in the schools. A conservative estimate for fiscal year 1998 would be $80,000.

In its first two years of operation, the Center received support from DeWitt Wallace–Reader's Digest Fund Incentive Awards in Teacher Education. These funds supported planning efforts, the initial teacher study groups, and the first two leadership associates programs. The awards required a double match, with one-third from the university and one-third from another source. A total of $375,000 supported the work of the Center for the first two years.

Of this, $75,000 was the university's match in the second year, and this became part of the base budget thereafter.

Enabling Conditions

The enabling conditions that follow helped to make the Center of Pedagogy a reality in the Montclair State University setting. These conditions may not be essential in every setting, but they played a critical role in this case.

An Appropriate Reward System and Relevant Scholarship

One structural element viewed as essential for the long-term success of a center of pedagogy is for the university to have a reward structure that values the kind of work that center faculty do. Montclair State University redesigned its reward system at the same time that its Center of Pedagogy evolved.

In a 1990 meeting of the faculty, the provost expressed his interest in exploring altered faculty loads, revised expectations for scholarship, and new conceptions of scholarship.[20] This announcement marked the beginning of long negotiations and discussions with the faculty union, conducted by the negotiating team of the administration, which included the dean of the College of Education and Human Services and the dean of the College of Science and Mathematics, who had strong mutual interest in the principles under discussion. Eventually, the state-level union challenged the right of the local union to negotiate an agreement that affected teaching loads, which are covered in the state contract. As a result, these negotiations were carried out informally. In 1994, with the support of the local union, the Montclair State University administration announced the FSIP and negotiated procedures for its implementation. Using Ernest Boyer's *Scholarship Reconsidered* as grounding,[21] the program offered faculty the opportunity to devote one-quarter of their load time to scholarship, newly defined, and to have decisions for reappointment, tenure, and promotion follow from their choices. Under the program, all faculty are evaluated using the following categories:

- *Teaching*—the most important function of a teaching university. All faculty are expected to teach during each academic year. Teaching includes not only traditional classroom, laboratory, and studio instruction, but also such activities such as the supervision of interns and student teachers and advising.

- *Scholarship of pedagogy*—designed to enhance teaching. Faculty strengthen their ability to "stimulate active, not passive, learning and encourage students to be critical, creative thinkers with the capacity to go on learning after their college days are over."[22]

- *Scholarship of discovery, integration, or aesthetic creation*—closest to the traditional forms of scholarship. Faculty in this area add to the knowledge base of their disciplines, make connections among existing ideas within or across disciplines, or produce works of art, including creative writing.

- *Scholarship of application*—the application of knowledge to issues of contemporary social concern. Faculty apply their disciplinary knowledge to strengthen the effectiveness of societal institutions, such as public schools, museums, or social agencies, as well as the quality of life on campus.[23]

Under FSIP, faculty may propose a scholarly project in one of the areas of pedagogy, discovery/integration/aesthetic creation, or application. After review by a faculty reader and chair, the dean has the final authority to approve proposals, which typically run over two years and provide up to one-quarter time for faculty to work on the project. The weighting system used to evaluate faculty is adjusted to emphasize the area of scholarship selected. Faculty who participate in the program may have only minimal released time for administration. (Any administrative time reduces their eligibility to participate in the program.) In addition, they must produce an interim and a final report, and they are expected to produce materials that are of such a quality that, "following peer review," they "are selected for dissemination through publications, reports, colloquia, conference presentations or other normally accepted venues for such presentations."[24]

The presence of this reward system, which applies to all colleges and schools of the university, has been extraordinarily beneficial in a number of ways to both the College of Education and Human Services and the Center of Pedagogy. First, schools in the NJNER can express an interest in collaboration with a university faculty member on research in a particular area of interest. These interests are made known to university faculty, and when a match of faculty interest and school interest is found, the faculty member can propose a project to which he or she would devote one-quarter time. Second, arrangements are made for at least one university faculty member with an FSIP project to be assigned to each professional development school and therefore to be present at least one-quarter time. On-site teaching and supervision typically increase load time devoted to the professional development school to one-half or more. Third, the renewal work at the core of the Center of Pedagogy is built into the reward system for faculty who pursue it. Fourth, the application of the reward system across the schools and colleges of the university makes the participation of arts and sciences faculty much more likely.

One criterion for the approval of projects is that they reflect the academic goals of the college. The academic goals of the College of Education and Human Services center on preparing professionals with the following capabilities:

- To examine their respective disciplines through critical thinking and to possess the requisite knowledge and skills to be practitioners within their profession

- To know how to make good judgments using critical thinking

- To understand the moral dimensions of their profession

- To assume the responsibility of being stewards of best practice within their profession

- To understand the role of educators in the enculturation of the young into a political and social democracy[25]

The overriding goal is to promote these capabilities within a program committed to the simultaneous renewal of the preparation of education professionals and the effectiveness of the professions in which they will serve. All proposals from College of Education faculty must show their relevance to these goals, which embody the shared vision of the NJNER and thus advance the mission of the college, especially as related to the Center of Pedagogy and the Agenda for Education in a Democracy.

As the university entered the fourth year of the program, approximately 60 percent of the faculty had chosen to participate.[26] There is evidence that faculty choosing nontraditional scholarship—that is, scholarship of application and pedagogy—are being offered tenure and are being promoted. The program was implemented with no additional funds, and was possible because of a reduction in administrative released time for faculty and a small increase in class size.[27] For the Center of Pedagogy, it provided access to up to one-quarter of the time of university faculty for renewal work.

The system does not, of course, reflect a reward system for faculty in P–12 schools, the third member group of the Center of Pedagogy. In many districts, faculty report strong support for their work, as districts honor their agreement to promote, support, and acknowledge the participation of faculty in NJNER work. Participating faculty are featured at school meetings and asked to assume leadership roles; generally they feel that their work is valued. In a few schools, faculty report some hostility from the colleagues who are not active in Center or NJNER activities. It seems that in some schools the actions of building administrators in highlighting the NJNER and Center have put participants at a disadvantage with their colleagues. In these instances, the university has worked to make certain that faculty understand that all who meet the criteria can join the NJNER and that it is not intended to be a small, elite group.

Clearly, for university faculty, the combination of being allowed time to do the work and having the work count substantially under the reward system is significant. Time for teachers in the P–12 settings is harder to free up, although many schools have used the presence of cohorts of student teachers—"junior faculty," they are called—to arrange for professional development time. The absence of a systematic reward structure for participating classroom teachers is a serious problem yet to be overcome; it seems to occur in many, if not most, university-school partnerships.[28] In part to address this issue of recognition for P–12 faculty, the faculty of the College of Education and Human Services, in collaboration with colleagues in the arts and sciences, developed a doctorate in education with a focus on pedagogy for classroom teachers, designed in part to make the highest academic degree available to classroom teachers who desire to be leaders without leaving the classroom. The program, housed in the Center of Pedagogy, was approved by the New Jersey Commission on Higher Education in October 1998. The hope is that this program will help in building appropriate reward opportunities for teachers. The National Board for Professional Teaching Standards has also been promoted as a vehicle to recognize excellence in teaching and to lead to more appropriate reward systems, and the need to reward excellent teaching is an important recommendation of the National Commission for Teaching & America's Future.[29]

Joint Appointments

The concept of a joint appointment between two academic departments is fairly common in higher education, but it did not exist at Montclair State University until 1996. Had the university decided to limit joint appointments to those between two academic departments, the negotiations with the faculty union would have been relatively simple and straightforward. However, administrators realized that appointment to units that are not academic departments in the traditional sense, such as the Center of Pedagogy and the university's Institute for Archaeology, would be desirable. Certainly, such appointments would be in the interest of the Center of Pedagogy. After several years of negotiations, the faculty adopted and ratified a plan that allows for such joint appointments. The advantage to faculty, especially in the arts and sciences, is that such a dual appointment guarantees administrative consideration of their work in teacher education because the Center of Pedagogy, through member faculty, has direct input into the processes of reappointment, tenure, and promotion for such faculty. Further, these joint appointments elevate the academic standing of the Center. Although joint appointments were not viewed as an essential prerequisite for the Center, and it is too soon to see tangible results in this setting, the concept has proven to be significant in other NNER settings.[30]

Support from the Administration

When Montclair's new president took note of the outreach efforts of the College of Education and Human Services, a new era of support and renewal began. Such support has continued and increased through two subsequent presidents and provosts. The president under whose watch the Center was established took office in 1988 and served until 1997, while the provost had been in his position since 1984. Both were strong supporters of the program in tangible ways. The president, for example, attended national conferences on critical thinking and participated at one such meeting on a panel discussing the role of critical thinking in teacher education. Both the provost and the president strongly supported the affiliation of the university with the NNER. At the initial meeting of the eight settings of the NNER in Seattle in the summer of 1991, the provost accompanied faculty and administrators from the College of Education and the schools to the meeting and participated enthusiastically in the deliberations. In fact, participation in the NNER has brought considerable recognition to the university, and both the provost and president view the work carried out by the Center of Pedagogy and the College of Education as on the cutting edge. This stature has led to a number of specific actions, including funding the Center, establishing tenure track lines for the directors of the NJNER and the Center, funding the associates program, appointing clinical faculty, assigning responsibility for the university's first doctoral program to the Center of Pedagogy, funding minority recruitment through the Teacher Education Advocacy Center, and instituting a reward system that recognizes work in schools.

There is no formula for developing this kind of support. Some elements of the mix are idiosyncratic to particular institutions. For example, the provost joined the university in the same year as the current dean of the College of Education and Human Services, and the two have a history of collaboration. The key for maintaining such support is continuing to deliver a program that is distinctive and is recognized for its excellence.

Reflections on the Future

The Center of Pedagogy is a work in progress. It is always moving toward hoped-for outcomes and looking ahead to possible future issues.

Networks

Networking is vital to the kind of complicated change that has occurred at Montclair State. The university was not alone in this endeavor; it was a member of two very supportive networks.

The NNER linked the university with other tripartite settings sharing similar (but not identical) agendas and missions. The common aspects of their agendas were shaped in part by the postulates Goodlad outlined in *Teachers for Our Nation's Schools*, which provided a set of conditions deemed necessary for educational renewal.[31] The comparable missions, with their moral dimensions, require a focus on access to knowledge, nurturing pedagogy, stewardship of best practice, and enculturation of the young into a political and social democracy, all within a context of simultaneous renewal. For Montclair State University, these basic forms of agenda and mission were amplified by the commitment to critical thinking, which led to a considerable broadening of the sources used to explore and understand the meaning of democracy. Nevertheless, there were other sites engaged in similar work. Deans from these sites, along with leadership associates from all tripartite groups, met regularly to discuss progress and problems, compare experiences, and offer support.

The second network, the NEA's Teacher Education Initiative, provided a set of principles that were consistent with the agenda and mission of the NNER, support for the gathering of data and assessment of progress, and help working within New Jersey's strong union context. Specifically, the NEA helped to build close ties with the New Jersey affiliate (the New Jersey Education Association) and helped to arrange meetings with union leaders in the NJNER districts. All NJNER districts but one are affiliates of NEA; the exception, Newark, is an affiliate of the AFT.

Networking provided external validation of the work going on inside the institution and partnership as well as support when problems were encountered.

The Shared Vision

The evolution of a shared vision was the most critical element in the renewal of teacher education at Montclair State University. The gradually developed position now embodied in the "Portrait of a Teacher"—with its roots in critical thinking, in the work of Goodlad and his associates (heavily rooted, of course, in the work of Dewey), and in the NEA Teacher Education Initiative—became the focal point for renewal. Without a substantive goal connected to what are believed to be the core purposes of education—student learning and citizenship—change efforts can easily become distracted and unfocused.

The shared vision continues to evolve. It must, for otherwise the quest for renewal will be lost. It evolves through the continuing work of task forces, annual advances, new cohorts of Leadership Associates, the addition of new NJNER districts, and interactions with new faculty and students who bring fresh perspectives. The differences between reform and renewal are many; most important, perhaps, is that renewal is ongoing, part of the fabric of an organization, while reform has a conclusion. It is renewal that keeps an organization alive. No other lesson in this experience has been more important.

Turf, Curricular Fragmentation, and Responsibility

That the Center of Pedagogy has provided a vehicle for finding common ground among the tripartite participants is evident in the recommendations of the Center's first task forces. These recommendations called for changes in the major sequence, the professional sequence, and the university's general education program in the best interest of preparing the nation's teachers rather than the interests of the turf that members of these task forces represented. In previous years, it would have been much more likely that recommendations would come from one element of the tripartite or another—not from a group representing all three. This unity makes the outcomes of the work of these task forces more palatable and politically more viable. Many of the recommendations have been implemented, contributing, along with the "Portrait of a Teacher," to making the curriculum more seamless and less fragmented.

There is substantial evidence that faculty in the arts and sciences and in the schools have taken responsibility for the quality of teacher education through the Center of Pedagogy. In one instance, a department chair from the College of Humanities and Social Sciences who had a strong interest in service-learning used his experience as a leadership associate to help frame a grant proposal to bring to the university service-learning with a primary focus on teacher education. His understanding of the role of the school in developing citizens, along with his close work with faculty in education, led to his leadership in bringing resources to teacher education that in another time would more likely have been driven by turf.

Another faculty member in the same college, also a leadership associate, became excited about the application of technology to teaching and engaged in major efforts to renew his own teaching using technology. At the beginning of an academic year, he offered to share his work at a faculty meeting of the College of Education and Human Services, to invite suggestions, and to form working groups to infuse technology throughout teacher education. He reported that he felt an affinity to faculty in the College of Education and Human Services.

Reconnecting Knowledge and Practice

Clearly, the Center of Pedagogy has benefited from the university's FSIP, but it has also helped to shape the program. The renewal work that was under way at the time that this program was being developed, largely in urban schools, gave credibility to faculty who were working in schools toward renewal. It is hard to tell how much that credibility was responsible for acceptance of the idea of crediting faculty time devoted to scholarship of application in schools; although an interest in working in other community settings was present in other parties to the agreement, the most concrete and successful examples extant at the time were in education.

Whatever credit teacher education activities may deserve for the shape of FSIP, it is clear that the redefinition of scholarship under way at Montclair and at many other institutions has helped to bridge the gap between knowledge and practice, making applied research and research on pedagogy central parts of the faculty reward system.

Leadership and Stability

One characteristic of Montclair State University that may partially explain its outcomes is the unusual stability of leadership. From 1988 until 1997, there was no change in president, provost, or dean of education at Montclair State. Nevertheless, there was change. For example, the director of teacher education, who was responsible for much of the initiative in moving renewal forward, left his position but continued to work to coordinate the NEA partnership. The directors of the NJNER and of the Center of Pedagogy were added during this period. After twenty-eight months, the first director of the Center of Pedagogy resigned, and a nationwide search followed for a replacement.

Change in all the positions is inevitable. It is hypothesized, however, that the vision and mission are so pervasive among the corps of individuals from education, the arts and sciences, and the schools who are active in these renewal efforts that any change in leadership will have a minimal impact on the ongoing work.

Status and Identity

Those associated with the College of Education and Human Services believe that the college is stronger for having shared its responsibilities with faculty in the schools and faculty in arts and sciences. One might wonder how giving so many of its resources to the Center of Pedagogy can make it stronger.

First, strength is not measured entirely in the accumulation of resources. The resources shared with other members of the tripartite were not lost to teacher education, and therefore not lost to the prime mission of the College of Education and Human Services.

Second, to be held responsible for outcomes without really controlling the factors leading to those outcomes places a person or institution in an inherently weak position. Many schools, colleges, and departments of education unfortunately find themselves in just that predicament. The education of future teachers is as much in the hands of faculty in the arts and sciences as it is in the hands of faculty in education—in most places, more. In addition, field experiences in the schools can make or break a teacher's perspective on his or her role and competence. The only way to achieve excellence in teacher education is for it to be the responsibility of all three groups, and at Montclair State, the Center of Pedagogy is the vehicle to achieve that end.

The College of Education and Human Services at Montclair State University is no longer solely responsible for the quality of teachers emerging from the university. Instead, the college can focus on issues regarding the purpose and mission of schooling in America, especially the public purpose; issues of nurturing pedagogy and stewardship; the cultural context of education; and the policy issues that support teaching and learning in a democracy. These are among the curricular areas that the faculty of a school, college, or department of education are best prepared and able to focus on, and these are the aspects of the preparation of educators for which they should be held accountable.

In this sense, because the College of Education and Human Services has a clearer and more realistic mission, role, and responsibility, and because it has joined with partners in the arts and sciences and the schools through the Center of Pedagogy, it is stronger and more likely to succeed.

Centers of pedagogy have been a long time coming. Some elements that are now reflected in them were recommended by Dewey and others; some have even been tried before. For example, Montclair State Teachers College in 1927 changed the name of the Department of Education to the Department of Integration, reflecting its function of "integrating subject matter, teaching technique, observation, practice, and other professional aspects of teaching."[32] The record does not show why or how that earlier experiment ended, or even how long it lasted. However, the time has come to extend the concept to recognize that the essential elements needed for the ongoing simultaneous renewal of the education of educators and the conditions and curricula of the schools can best be put in place through a center of pedagogy. The prospects for the success of the concept have never been better, and the need for the renewal of education in our democracy has seldom been greater.

Brigham Young University, Utah

In 1996, at the celebration of the seventy-fifth anniversary of the College of Education at Brigham Young University (BYU), the university's academic vice president announced that the board of trustees had given official approval for the creation of a unit to be known as CITES: the Center for the Improvement of Teacher Education and Schooling. Since 1984 the College of Education had been involved in a partnership with five neighboring school districts, dedicated to the simultaneous renewal of teacher education and public schooling. Through a wide variety of collaborative projects between the university and the schools, a high degree of mutual trust had developed. Now the partnership was in the process of expanding to include arts and sciences departments across the university. With the increased numbers of stakeholders and the increased complexity of programs and projects, it became evident that there was a need for a new administrative structure, one that could encourage, facilitate, and coordinate the collaborative processes involving all three of these partners. Administrators in the College of Education, influenced strongly by John Goodlad's notion of a center of pedagogy, had proposed the plan for CITES in order to fulfill these needs.

As an anniversary tribute, the central administration and board of trustees of the university gave their approval to establish the Center. In pledging their administrative and monetary support, these governing groups affirmed their belief that teacher education should be central among the programs at the university. In addition, they recognized and supported the need of the university for such a center to coordinate teacher education components that existed throughout other colleges and departments in the institution and to draw all of these units into the partnership with the public schools.

The decision to establish CITES resulted from careful study of institutional needs and of ways that had been proposed for meeting those particular needs. As one of the sixteen school-university partnerships in the National Network for Educational Renewal (NNER), the Brigham Young University–Public School Partnership (BYU-PSP) had long been influenced by the thinking of Goodlad and his associates in the Center for Educational Renewal. Since the early 1990s, when this group began espousing centers of pedagogy as administrative units for providing governance and direction to teacher education,[1] BYU had closely followed their development in the literature and in practice. Having introduced the concept in *Teachers for Our Nation's Schools*, Goodlad advocated these centers as a way "to bring to the fore the centrality and clarity of the teacher education mission in a democratic society."[2] Centers of pedagogy were to be committed to the simultaneous renewal of teacher education and schooling, a proposition central to the operation of the BYU-PSP, and they were to extend the partnership of the teacher preparation unit and the public schools to include cross-campus affiliates, a relationship that BYU had found to be particularly challenging in recent years. Goodlad warned that to propose this three-way collaboration was to ask "for what has not been and will not easily be."[3] But those in BYU's College of Education felt the need for this form of collaboration, understood its potential value, and were willing to take risks and work creatively in order to achieve it.

As CITES approached its second anniversary in 1998, it was still seeking to understand and fulfill its potential. Indeed, many in the BYU-PSP still did not understand why it existed and what it did. This chapter's brief recounting of BYU-PSP's history and examination of its underlying structures and principles both confirm its value and potential and display some of its many projects and services that have proven beneficial both to the university and to the schools in the partnership districts.

Each university or school-university partnership is unique in its setting, needs, resources, relationships, and administrative support, and the organizational structures appropriate for each will vary. However, many of the experiences and insights that participants have gained from the development of CITES can be generalized to a variety of institutions that are seeking means for effecting simultaneous change in teacher preparation and public school quality.

The Setting for the Center

Fundamental to understanding and appreciating a structure like CITES is an understanding of the context in which it has developed. Some of the unique conditions at BYU make the institution particularly suited to a center of pedagogy such as Goodlad proposed.

Brigham Young University is a private university sponsored by the Church of Jesus Christ of Latter-day Saints. Situated at the foot of the Wasatch Mountains in Provo, Utah, approximately forty-five miles south of Salt Lake City, BYU has a full-time student population of nearly twenty-eight thousand. Although classified according to the Carnegie system of ranking as a Research I university, BYU is primarily an undergraduate institution, with approximately twenty-five thousand of its students in undergraduate programs. Degrees are offered in eleven different colleges and schools, and students come from all fifty states and from 102 foreign countries.

Because it is funded by the Church of Jesus Christ of Latter-day Saints, independent of public support from either state or federal sources, BYU serves a predominantly church population. Students are expected to abide by an honor code and to take courses in religion in addition to their other academic studies. The common religious values shared by most of the students, regardless of major or profession, include the importance of educating and nurturing children and youths. This mind-set concerning the importance of teaching and learning has been instrumental in obtaining cross-campus support for the development of CITES.

Teacher Education Units

In 1875, Brigham Young Academy was created as both a high school and a normal school to prepare teachers for what was predominantly a religious community. Historically, teacher education has been prominent at BYU, and today roughly four thousand students have declared a major in teacher education. Annually, more than a thousand students graduate with a bachelor's degree in early childhood, elementary, or secondary education.

Degrees in early childhood and elementary education are granted by the David O. McKay School of Education (formerly the College of Education) through the Department of Teacher Education. Graduate degrees can be obtained in the Department of Teacher Education and through four other departments in the School of Education: Audiology and Speech Language Pathology, Counseling and Special Education, Educational Leadership and Foundations, and Instructional Psychology and Technology. The five departments house ninety-two full-time faculty.

Secondary teacher certification is spread across eight of the eleven colleges and schools of the university, with approximately thirty full-time faculty who specialize in curriculum, instruction, and teacher education but are hired by and housed in different campus departments. The degrees in secondary education are offered by the individual departments, colleges, and schools, but the dean of the School of Education is responsible for recommending candidates for certification. All teacher education programs at the university are accredited by both the Utah state Office of Education and the National Council for Accreditation of Teacher Education; yet there has been lack of consistency and articulation across the programs because communication among the departments has been limited in scope and extent.

Brigham Young University–Public School Partnership

In 1983, John Goodlad, who had been dean of the Graduate School of Education at the University of California at Los Angeles and was in the process of moving to the University of Washington to become director of the new Center for Educational Renewal, agreed to assist BYU in establishing an official partnership between the College of Education and five local school districts. Within a year the partnership was in place. When Goodlad formed the first NNER in 1986, the BYU-PSP became one of the initial ten members. The NNER was reconstituted in 1991, and again the BYU-PSP was accepted for membership.

The five districts in the BYU-PSP enroll approximately one-third of the schoolchildren in the state of Utah. Jordan School District, the largest of the five, has a student population of nearly seventy thousand. The other four districts—Alpine, Nebo, Provo, and Wasatch—range from four thousand students to forty-five thousand. The districts vary in their size and in the nature of the communities that they serve; however, they share common concerns for providing optimal education for children, and they have shown remarkable willingness to collaborate and to pursue a shared agenda with the university.

The structure and shared goals of the BYU-PSP have enabled it to move easily through changes in leadership at the university and in the districts. During the twelve years of partnership operation, the superintendents in all the districts have changed at least once, the College (now School) of Education has had four deans, and the university has had three presidents. But for all of the partners, commitment has been stable, and activity has increased.

From its inception until the development of CITES, the BYU-PSP was regulated by a governing board consisting of the superintendents of the five districts and the dean of the School of Education. The board has met monthly, with each of the participants having an equal vote. An executive director takes care of such operational matters as budget, liaison work among districts and with the university and the state Office of Education, and planning and development.

Development of the Center

The size and complexity of Brigham Young University and the BYU-PSP, as well as the diversity involved in its teacher education programs, necessitated a structure that would facilitate communication and collaboration among the diverse units. But ascertaining the specific needs to be met by the structure and securing the cooperation of various cross-campus units seemed almost impossible. However, a series of conditions and administrative requests, which at first seemed to be an awkward burden to the College of Education, proved to be opportunities for both the necessary analysis and the ensuing communication.

A Window of Opportunity

An unanticipated window of opportunity to propose a center of pedagogy grew out of discussions and planning associated with an accreditation review of BYU by the Northwest Accreditation Association. In 1994 the central administration announced that all colleges, schools, and departments within the university would undertake a rigorous self-study as the first step in preparing for the review. The initial self-studies would expand into long-range planning studies, providing the university with data requisite for a fundamental review of programs, services, and operations, in addition to the material necessary for the accreditation process. All units within the university found the process intense and grueling, but all were able to provide the requested information within a surprisingly short time. These reports were analyzed and critiqued by a self-study committee from the central administration, as well as the accreditation review team, and extensive recommendations were given concerning priorities, needs, resources, programs, and physical facilities.

For those involved in teacher education, the process revealed many inefficiencies and needs, and its ramifications were consequential. Secondary teacher preparation was especially problematic. Because students received degrees through the departments of their subject specialization, the secondary program was spread across thirty academic departments and eight colleges or schools. Although the dean of the College of Education had been given responsibility for recommending all teacher education candidates to the state for certification, this charge did not carry with it any stewardship or authority to oversee the quality of the various teacher preparation programs from which the students were to be recommended. The quality of the programs, commitment and interest of the faculty, and allocation of resources were the responsibilities of a varied group of deans and department chairs from throughout the university. Across more than thirty-eight administrative units, these aspects of support varied considerably. In some units, dedicated personnel assigned to teacher preparation worked hard and efficiently. In others, administrators and faculty were less concerned. In a number of departments, resources formerly allocated for teacher education positions had been transferred to new departmental priorities. Interest in and willingness to cooperate with local schools varied considerably among the departments.

BYU's situation was typical of the conditions that Goodlad and his associates had found in their studies of teacher education across the United States. As was the case in many other institutions that had originally been founded as normal schools dedicated to the preparation of teachers, BYU had lost sight of its roots as a result of its rapid growth and new priorities. The leaders in the College of Education found in the nineteen postulates Goodlad articulated in *Teachers for Our Nation's Schools* an accurate portrayal of the needs that had to be met in order to accomplish what they desired at BYU.

Preliminary discussions and planning activities of the Accreditation and Long-Range Planning Committee provided the dean of education an opportunity to prepare a position paper on teacher education to inform the committee of the problems facing teacher education and to make a few suggestions for remedial action. At this time he called attention to the potential advantages of a center of pedagogy, as described by Goodlad in his books *Teachers for Our Nation's Schools* and *Educational Renewal: Better Teachers, Better Schools*. Fortuitously, the ideas in *Educational Renewal* became available at just the time when they could be presented and considered within the context of the accreditation study at BYU.

A center of pedagogy, supported by a few structural changes within the College of Education, would have the potential to coordinate teacher education across the departments and colleges of the university and at the same time encourage and sustain collaborative activities of those units with the education faculty and with teachers in the school districts of the BYU-PSP.

Developmental Uncertainties and Progress

The difficulty of bringing the total teacher education community within the university to an understanding and appreciation of the idea of a center of pedagogy actually illustrated the need for such a center. Stakeholders were spread throughout the university and the public schools, and there was no unit or procedure to bring them together in the type of conversation required to establish consensus and support. Efforts had to be spread through a variety of contexts.

Meetings were held with all the deans whose units had any responsibility for teacher education. The deans had to be convinced that there was a need for a coordinating structure within teacher education and for more effective linking of the university groups with the public schools. Emphasis was placed on the joint ownership of teacher education, a concept that was not comfortable for some of the subject-area specialists. Some did not want to lose what they considered their autonomy and control over teacher education in their subject specialties. Some feared that an "unholy alliance" with the College of Education would be forced on them; they lacked respect for the education faculty and programs and were concerned that the association would be an embarrassment to them. In contrast, other units were pleased with the proposal for the center, feeling that the prospect of collaboration would overcome what they believed to be unilateral control of teacher education by the College of Education. They were surprised that the college was willing to open its courses and programs to scrutiny and review within the center.

It was possible to reassure those who were anxious about losing control of their programs that the new center would not be a means of wresting authority away from departments or of aggrandizing the College of Education. However, there seemed to be no easy way to dispel the negative view that many had of the education professors and administration. Rather than argue that such a view was unwarranted or that conditions had changed considerably since the view was initially formed, the college attempted to focus on the common desire that teacher education across the institution should be of exceptionally high quality and that it should be owned by all.

Just as the proposal and ensuing discussions seemed to be opening the way for the center of pedagogy, the death of the university's president caused uncertainty over the future of the endeavor. The center, along with other proposed changes in the institution, came under additional scrutiny as the new administration endeavored to simplify and refocus university governance and programs. Though sometimes frustrating, the necessity of describing, defending, and legitimating the center proved to be worthwhile. Several months of exchanging ideas, in meetings and on paper, heightened understanding of the need for the center and increased commitment to the center specifically and to teacher education generally on the part of the university administration. Both the departing and the incoming academic vice presidents approved the university's matching a $50,000 grant from the DeWitt Wallace–Reader's Digest Fund Incentive Award in Teacher Education, also matched by the Utah state superintendent of education, for establishing the center of pedagogy.

Although the window of opportunity for the center had occurred as the need for uniting the disparate aspects of teacher education at the university had been revealed, the purpose of the center was to integrate public school colleagues into the decisions and programs as well. CITES had been conceived as a means for achieving three-way collaboration, and winning the support of the district superintendents was as important as winning the support of the university administration and departments. The BYU-PSP had been functioning for over ten years, most of that time in affiliation with the NNER. During that time, the districts had actively supported joint initiatives for improving preservice and inservice teacher preparation, curriculum development, and education research. Two of the five superintendents had participated in the Leadership Associates Program that Goodlad and his colleagues led at the Institute for Educational Inquiry in Seattle. Through this experience they had developed trust in their university colleagues and in the strength of collaboration.

Although the dean of education was able to outline only a loosely defined concept for the center in his initial presentation to the BYU-PSP governing board, the superintendents readily endorsed the proposal and subsequently agreed to provide the necessary support from their districts to enable the state superintendent to provide the second matching grant required for receipt of the DeWitt Wallace–Reader's Digest Incentive Award funding. These superintendents understood the need for a new structure, and they trusted that a new and appropriate form would emerge. A decade of working together had engendered and reinforced this kind of trust. At annual conferences of the BYU-PSP in 1995 and 1996, discussions of the proposed center were included. In addition, the BYU-PSP's first Associates Retreat (1995–1996) addressed the same topic and promoted support.

All of the presentations and discussions of the center met with a common dilemma: the organizational problems necessitating a center were easy to recognize, but the proposed structure lacked clear role definition. The lack of a carefully crafted description of the structure and operation of the proposed center caused a sense of uneasiness, particularly in some areas of the university, and to a lesser extent among some participants from the BYU-PSP. Those who had reservations or even suspicions about the center spoke openly and critically. Although the university's self-study process had opened the window of opportunity to establish the need for a center of pedagogy and prepare a proposal, some aspects of the process proved to be a hindrance. The proposal could not be developed and refined through the customary channels of deliberation and approval at the university. Greater understanding and ownership of the center across the faculty in the university and in the schools would have been possible if the self-study had not fragmented and narrowed the focus of attention of the various units as the proposal was being developed.

The College of Education celebrated its seventy-fifth anniversary a year after receiving the DeWitt Wallace–Reader's Digest Fund Incentive Award along with the required matching grants from the university and the state office. As part of the anniversary celebration, the college announced significant changes in its structure and administration. Departments would be realigned, with the formerly separate departments housing early childhood, elementary, and secondary education combining into a Department of Teacher Education, a structure that would promote unity and consistency among the programs, facilitating increased participation of preservice teachers in the public schools. The name *College of Education* was changed to *School of Education*, emphasizing the similarities between teacher preparation and the professional preparation provided by schools of law, business, nursing, and others. In addition, the status of "school" would allow the unit greater autonomy within the university structure than had the former "college" designation. Along with these changes, facilitating them and being in turn facilitated by them, the Center for the Improvement of Teacher Education and Schooling (CITES) was formally initiated and approved.

Current Functions and Characteristics of CITES

During its first two years of operation, CITES has undertaken a variety of projects and initiatives. Much can be learned by examining its structure and operations. Though many of its characteristics are unique to the BYU setting and many functions are specialized to the needs of the local Utah context, much can still be generalized to other university–public school partnerships in a wide range of circumstances.

Strategies and Objectives

The Center for the Improvement of Teacher Education and Schooling adopted the following strategies and objectives:

- Fostering and sustaining the tripartite involvement of the School of Education, the cross-campus departments of the arts and sciences, and the personnel of partnership public schools in planning and providing teacher education programs

- Examining and promoting moral purposes shared by these participants as the foundation of both public schooling and teacher preparation

- Encouraging and facilitating the development of partner schools as exemplary learning communities for students, teachers, and university faculty

- Maintaining membership in the NNER and sustaining relationships with other NNER settings, the Center for Educational Renewal, and the Institute for Educational Inquiry

- Seeking, acquiring, and distributing resources to colleagues across the university and in the schools to support inquiry, program development, and school renewal

- Encouraging and supporting inquiry, including program evaluation, as a means of building a credible foundation of knowledge for the purpose of improving teacher education and schooling

Tripartite Involvement and Responsibility

For the first ten years of the BYU-PSP, the collaboration between schools and the university had centered primarily on elementary schools, elementary teacher education programs, and a leadership preparation program for principals. The secondary schools and the arts and sciences departments of the university that prepared secondary teachers, including curriculum and instruction specialists, did not work collaboratively with each other and were limited in their collaboration with teacher education faculty. Student teaching placements were arranged with a few teachers, but ownership and control of teacher preparation was largely centered in the university departments.

The notion that governance and operation of teacher education should involve professors from the School of Education and teachers practicing in the public schools in addition to the subject-area specialists has been a challenge to the established cultural hierarchy of university and schools. Although the rhetoric has come to favor terms like *joint ownership* and *interdependence*, deeply entrenched behaviors and attitudes are difficult to overcome. One of the primary functions of CITES has been to help school and university personnel discover and accept Goodlad's perspective:

> For schools to get better, they must have better teachers, among other things. To prepare better teachers (and counselors, special educators, and administrators) universities must have access to school settings exhibiting the very best practices. To assure the best practices, schools must have ongoing access to alternative ideas and knowledge. For universities to have access to exemplary settings and for these settings to become and remain exemplary, the schools and the preparing institutions must develop symbiotic relationships through joining together as equal partners. In the kind of partnership envisioned,

universities have a stake in and responsibility for school improvement just as the schools have an interest in and responsibility for the education of those who will staff the schools.[4]

Common Moral Purposes

Efforts to design teacher education programs commonly fail to consider moral purposes that should guide the role of teachers in today's society. As a result, debates about content and pedagogy become confused, and questions of instrumentality are mistaken for those of ends or purpose. It is imperative that programs for the preparation of teachers consider the mission of schooling and the moral dimensions that permeate it. A four-part mission, infused with moral dimensions, has given direction to the work of CITES:

1. Enculturating the young in a social and political democracy
2. Providing access to the knowledge effective humans require
3. Teaching in a nurturing way
4. Exercising moral stewardship of schools[5]

Exemplary Partner Schools

Partner schools are the laboratories of the BYU-PSP within which ideas and methodologies for renewal are examined, discussed, practiced, and observed. All schools in the partnership districts benefit from the knowledge and experience that come from partnership participation, but only a few schools in each district have the dedication and desire to be part of the intense participation and experimentation that take place in the designated partner (or professional development) schools. Faculty and administrators in these schools commit to a change agenda focused on preservice teacher education, inservice teacher development, collaborative school-university inquiry projects, and constructive curriculum change. Insights and knowledge are disseminated through a variety of partnership conferences, presentations, and publications so that the benefits of the partner schools can be extended and shared.

Establishing and maintaining quality partner schools present numerous challenges. Where they act as collaboration centers for school and university personnel, they represent what might be called overlapping sovereignty. Although partner schools are under the basic governance structure of the school districts of which they are a part, latitude must be granted so that the university may participate in ways not common to school experience. CITES assumes an important role in identifying, establishing, and refining the functions of the various partner schools as they must meet the needs of the School of Education faculty and the arts and sciences faculty from the university without sacrificing the needs of the teachers and students within the school. The challenge inherent in balancing the interests of the various groups within each partner school is a microcosm of the balancing that CITES must do among these same groups as they function within the larger educational community. Partner schools are critical to the overall function of CITES and of the BYU-PSP as a whole.

Relationship with the National Network for Educational Renewal

The long-term relationship of the BYU-PSP with the NNER has resulted in varied and extensive benefits to the partnership, benefits that constantly expand and increase. The literature, presentations, and activities of the NNER, including those coming out of the Center for Educational Renewal and the Institute for Educational Inquiry, have produced and communicated the foundational ideas now known as the Agenda for Education in a Democracy— ideas at the very core of the formation and activities of the BYU-PSP. Professional development, leadership training, consultative help, financial support, and network visits and conversation have been vital components of the relationship.

An important benefit of the relationship between the BYU-PSP and the NNER has been the opportunity to share the ideas and insights generated through the activity of the partnership and of

CITES. Articulating their experiences allows BYU-PSP participants to learn from those experiences, and the feedback from other NNER settings has been invaluable.

Resource Acquisition and Distribution

CITES does not currently have a budget sufficient to allow it to make financial contributions to research or development. But because of its nature as a center for collaboration, it does have the capability to broker substantial and varied resources. By offering its approval and encouragement to projects, it can help individuals or groups to leverage funds that might otherwise be unavailable to them. For example, over a three-year period the BYU-PSP has obtained nearly $2 million of funding from Goals 2000, a federal initiative that provides grants for projects that will enhance professional development for educators. Individuals from throughout the BYU-PSP are invited to submit ideas; the governing board of the partnership selects those projects that will be taken to the State Office of Education, through which the funding is dispensed. Successful Goals 2000 projects have included a K–2 partnership-wide study and implementation of balanced literacy, two projects for English as a Second Language (K–2 and 3–6), a science endorsement program, a high school professional development program, and various inquiry initiatives to be carried out in professional development schools. In addition, participating partnership organizations have given funding and released time for essential personnel, coordinated by partnership personnel now under CITES leadership. By helping to obtain funds and other resources to support various projects, CITES also helps to clarify the goals and priorities behind these projects. One of the challenges that CITES has planned for the future is to seek and obtain funds from foundations and government entities.

Encouragement and Support for Inquiry

When groups or individuals are challenged by a schedule requiring them to build relationships, foster trust, undertake curricular planning, and encourage professional development, it can be easy to neglect or minimize engaging in research. Too often those involved in renewal activities rely on personal insight and knowledge derived from their own experience but largely uninformed by critical inquiry or systematic study. If teacher education and schooling are to be improved in significant and lasting ways, the change efforts must be founded on a credible knowledge base and supported by valid investigation.

Because it encourages and supports research, CITES has the potential for a dual contribution. First, it can add to the knowledge base of the profession in several important areas. Program evaluation studies can help establish critical dimensions for teacher education curricula. Inquiry into the nature of student learning can provide foundations for instructional methods as well as curriculum. As noted in Chapters Two and Three, exploring the collaborative processes that involve different educational organizations can assist the growth of more effective partnerships. Second, CITES's commitment to support inquiry can demonstrate the value of basing professional change and growth on an accepted and proven foundation of research rather than on idiosyncratic, arbitrary judgments and claims.

Organization and Governance

CITES does not control or exercise authority in a typical sense; rather, it coordinates through persuasion, through inviting and building consensus among participants in various units within the university and in the schools. It does not seek to alter or diminish organizational entities such as departments, colleges, school districts, or schools. Administrators within CITES recognize that collaboration cannot be mandated or legislated; it must be entered by choice, with a conviction that the benefits of the relationship are sufficiently compelling to cause participants to surrender a degree of their own autonomy in the interest of the common good. The establishment of CITES is an attempt to build a community of educators across the university and schools who do not feel threatened or diminished by collaboration, a community sustained by an unwritten social contract into which educators have entered of their own volition to promote shared ideas, beliefs, and commitments. Neither university nor school faculty have their permanent academic home in CITES; they remain members and citizens of their original academic or administrative units. Curricular programs also retain their traditional places in departments, colleges, and school districts.

In addition to respecting the allegiance of personnel and the turf involved with programs and developments, CITES recognizes traditional lines of authority within school districts and the university. Providing lines whereby ideas and practices are shared horizontally by participants from the different units does not erase the vertical lines by which authority and governance are maintained within them. CITES was created to build a new cultural perspective centered on collaborative relationships and commitment. Its fundamental premise is that interdisciplinary and interinstitutional collaboration can and will occur among reasonable people if the advantages of the collaboration are demonstrated, encouraged, and supported.

Management and Operation

During its first two years of operation, CITES grew considerably in the scope of its undertaking. This growth is evidence that both the university and the school districts were discovering the effectiveness of CITES in bringing the disparate groups involved in teacher education together in worthwhile ventures concerning teacher education and public school renewal. The organization, management, and scope of the agenda continue to be reexamined and altered to maintain appropriate levels of quality.

Management Structure

The business and activities of CITES are determined by a governing board, consisting of eight members in addition to an executive director. (Figure 5.1 outlines the organizational and management structure of CITES.) Board members are the superintendents of the five school districts of the partnership, the Utah state superintendent of education, BYU's associate academic vice president for undergraduate education, and the dean of the McKay School of Education. The chairperson who presides over the board is elected by the members. The executive director of the board and the director of CITES prepare the agendas for the monthly meetings. Each primary partner constituency is represented, with the university's associate academic vice president for undergraduate education representing the colleges and departments of the arts and sciences. Because all decisions must be reached by consensus, the number of representatives need not be equal between the school districts and the university units.

In order to ensure a direct link to the governance structure of the university and to assure the deans of cross-campus colleges and schools that the university interest will not be sacrificed by the representation from the school districts, the dean of the McKay School of Education is currently serving as the first director of CITES. A full-time executive director handles day-to-day operations and works with the director in preparing agendas for the meetings of the Executive Management Team and the Teacher Education Committee.

Leadership and direction for the various CITES initiatives are provided by the Executive Management Team, consisting of the director, the two executive directors, and six appointees: two from the school districts, two from the campus disciplines of the arts and sciences, and two from the McKay School of Education. The composition of this group was chosen to reflect the tripartite membership and goals of CITES. Currently, a Spanish literature professor and a physical chemist represent the arts and sciences departments—visible evidence of the importance of cross-campus disciplines in the conception and function of CITES. Each member of this team assumes responsibilities as "chief worrier" for specific agenda items

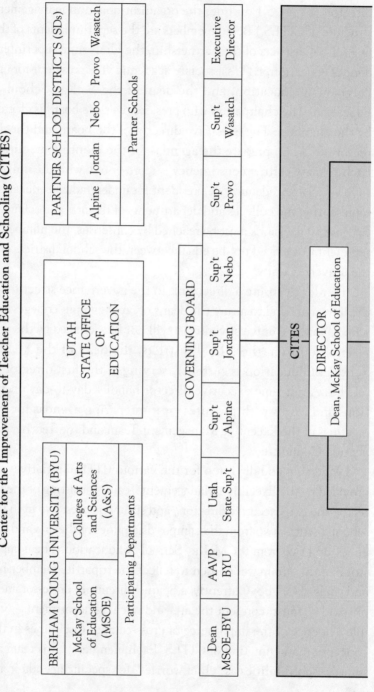

Figure 5.1. Organization and Management Schema of the
Center for the Improvement of Teacher Education and Schooling (CITES)

EXECUTIVE MANAGEMENT TEAM

Exec Dir	Exec Dir, CITES	MSOE Rep 1	MSOE Rep 2	A&S Rep 1	A&S Rep 2	SD Rep 1	SD Rep 2

TEACHER EDUCATION COMMITTEE

Executive Management Team	8–5 Associate Deans 3–5 SD Reps

AGENDA PRIORITY ITEMS

Tripartite Involvement	Moral Dimensions	Exemplary Partner Schools	National Network for Educational Renewal	Resources	Inquiry

Simultaneous Improvement of Teacher Education and School Renewal

PROJECTS AND ACTIVITIES

Preservice Teacher Education	Inservice Teacher Education	Spanish	Curriculum	ESL Distance Delivery	Inquiry
Secondary Education Restructuring	ESL Endorsement		K–2 Literacy 3–6 Literacy		Program Evaluation Elementary Education

RELATED PERSONNEL

Associates	Fellows	Professors of Pedagogy

Note: AAVP = associate academic vice president; Sup't = superintendent.

that emerge as the business of CITES. They meet monthly to propose, organize, and lead initiatives related to the CITES goals.

The members of the Executive Management Team also serve on the Teacher Education Committee. Chaired by the director of CITES, the committee includes three additional representatives of the partner school districts and an associate dean or counterpart from each college that is involved with teacher education, in addition to the Utah state Office of Education certification officer. This committee considers and makes official recommendations on all curriculum, program, and policy matters that the university's Curriculum Committee will eventually review. The deliberations and recommendations of the Teacher Education Committee provide an opportunity to explore matters related to Goodlad's nineteen postulates, among other concerns and dispositions associated with the purposes and function of CITES.

Seminars

For the purposes of examining common moral purposes and reconfirming the value of tripartite responsibility for teacher education and school renewal, CITES has undertaken two types of seminars. Both have been successful in initiating constituent groups within the university, the Utah state Department of Education, and the public schools into the many parts of the work of CITES.

A year before CITES was established, the BYU-PSP began laying groundwork by establishing a leadership associates program modeled on the program of the Institute for Educational Inquiry in Seattle. The first of the seminars included eighteen participants from across the university, the five school districts, and the state Office of Education. It met four times during the year, in a resort setting not far from BYU, to explore a set of readings and issues similar to those studied by the Seattle Associates group. After CITES was established, it extended this activity considerably. During its first year of operation, CITES conducted two seminars, or cohorts: one for personnel from the total BYU-PSP and one primarily for the

Alpine School District. A year later, six groups were organized to meet throughout the year: four in the partner school districts and two for the BYU-PSP overall.[6] Participating principals and faculty from one or two schools subsequently began to use a modified form of the model to promote professional growth in their individual schools.

The success of these associates programs has created some challenges for the management team of CITES. Quality leadership must be provided for this large number of groups, and increased funding has been necessary to provide for the ever-increasing number of participants. These challenges are being considered collaboratively, and creative solutions are being sought. A second need that has emerged from the success of the leadership associates programs is for ways to sustain interest and conversation among participants after the series of seminars has concluded. One response has been to hold an annual conference for all former participants. Currently some groups are looking for ways to engage former associates more frequently and more intensively in order to sustain and extend the conversations begun during the seminars.

In addition, CITES has held two-day seminars twice annually for deans and associate deans, superintendents and their administrative officers, and the state superintendent of education and one or two senior staff—approximately thirty people in all. During these seminars, administrators examine ways they can work together as well as individually in their respective spheres of responsibility to improve teacher education and schooling.

Curricular Activities

One of the projects CITES has undertaken is a major literacy initiative for all kindergarten through grade 2 teachers in the five partner school districts. The five district superintendents agreed that the most significant need in their schools was for curriculum enhancement and staff development in the area of literacy. They committed to a four- to five-year primary curriculum focus on literacy, including both the competency of their teachers and the development of their students' literacy skills. When completed, this project will extend the ideas until all K–2 faculty throughout the five districts are involved.

Even in its early stages, the literacy focus has demonstrated how CITES helps to facilitate collaboration and to spread knowledge. The literacy faculty of the David O. McKay School of Education agreed to join the school districts in this renewal effort, ensuring that prospective teachers graduating from BYU would have a perspective on teaching reading similar to that being promoted in the schools throughout the five partnership districts. Seven university faculty and twenty-five teachers and administrators from the five school districts began studying together and collaborating to develop a balanced approach to literacy that would be practicable in the partnership schools. They received released time from the districts and the university to carry out this work. At the end of the year of study and development, each of these thirty-two professionals began to engage ten teachers from the districts in a year or two of study to equip them with a similar, balanced literacy background. Each teacher, in turn, will work with one or two colleagues in the schools to share information and skills. The activity illustrates the extent of involvement that is possible when there is shared commitment on a common interest, coordinated by and facilitated through the structure of CITES. Inquiry is the initial step, as the earliest leader-participants study, reflect on, and report their own learning and development. Both teacher preparation and public schooling benefit from the analysis and sharing of the inquiry results.

Schools in the BYU-PSP have also emphasized the need for teachers to be better prepared to work with children who are learning English as a Second Language (ESL). CITES obtained approximately $500,000 through the state Office of Education, the BYU Continuing Education Department, the McKay School of Education, and the five partner districts to prepare six courses for video delivery that would qualify teachers for an ESL endorsement. CITES is accomplishing this project with two significant goals: to meet the increasing need for ESL teachers and to explore uses of technology in providing professional development opportunities.

Other projects undertaken during CITES's first years of operation pertained to Spanish, science, and mathematics. The chair of the BYU Spanish Department, who has been an Associate in the Institute for Educational Inquiry's Leadership Program, led his department in collaborating with teachers in three local high schools to improve the teaching of Spanish. These collaborators have formed a partnership within the partnership to explore such topics as concurrent enrollment in high school and university, professional development of high school teachers, and school-university personnel exchange. Several science faculty in the university have been working with science teachers in the districts to strengthen instruction in science. For example, the professor who directs use of the university's electron microscope works with both elementary and secondary students and teachers on special projects to develop student interest in science. This same professor encourages greater participation in science fairs as a way of stimulating interest in active science learning. In addition, the physical scientist on the CITES management team, who has also been an Institute for Educational Inquiry Leadership Associate, has joined with two science colleagues to initiate a project designed to engage schoolteachers and their students in the university professors' laboratory work. Two professors from the Department of Mathematics have received a grant of $20,000, plus money from CITES, to study how teachers and students acquire and use mathematical knowledge and skills.

An important emphasis of CITES is inquiry into ideas and practices of pedagogy. Three part-time professorships have been made available to university and school faculty members to assist them in pursuing research, conducting seminars, and publishing. A book on the role of positive tensions in school-university partnerships has come to press as a result of the first of these appointments.[7] Like the Institute for Educational Inquiry and the Center for Educational Renewal at the University of Washington, which have been idea centers for the NNER and other groups interested in school renewal, these professorships of pedagogy are intended to stimulate thought on renewal issues within the BYU-PSP.

New Structures

Revising and restructuring teacher education curricula for early childhood, elementary, and secondary education have been major undertakings for CITES. A restructured elementary education program through which preservice teachers spend their days in the schools both participating in classrooms and taking their methods courses on site was launched a year before CITES began operation. CITES has taken over extensive data collection and evaluation for this program.

Before CITES, the early childhood education program at BYU had been conducted in the College of Family, Home, and Social Sciences. Inconsistencies and a lack of understanding between the early childhood and elementary education programs had caused confusion, redundancies, and time loss for students who wanted to obtain dual certification in elementary and early childhood education. During its first full year of operation, CITES brought together university personnel from the School of Education and the Early Childhood Education Department, along with practitioners from the settings and kindergartens that had been providing practicum sites for the early childhood majors. The early childhood education program was moved to the David O. McKay School of Education to facilitate collaboration, and a new program was developed to provide an efficient and time- and cost-effective double major for preservice teachers who desire the flexibility of dual certification. A worthwhile development that illustrates the potential of cross-campus collaboration through CITES is preliminary discussion for a new course that would integrate art, music, dance, and drama for early childhood teachers.

Another major restructuring effort of CITES involves rebuilding the curriculum for secondary teacher education. Bringing together over thirty campus departments and countless secondary schools is a formidable challenge. But the project moves forward, with four high schools in the area having received Arthur Vining Davis grants to pursue new links with the university. One of the four schools is acting as an experimental site to study the feasibility of grouping secondary education students in a variety of majors into cohorts to move jointly through their curriculum experience.

Budget and Facilities

When CITES was formally announced in the fall of 1996, no permanent budget was awarded, and no specific space was designated for it. Thus far, the absence of established budgetary support has not been an insurmountable problem. The university, the school districts, the state superintendent, and the McKay School of Education have each provided grants of $50,000 to $75,000 to match the DeWitt Wallace–Reader's Digest Fund Incentive Awards given through the Institute for Educational Inquiry. These grants have totaled $625,000 over two years, and an additional $20,000 was added later to launch and sustain CITES and fund several of its key projects.

Additional resources for specific projects have been garnered from other sources. In each of the first two years, over $400,000 was acquired through Goals 2000 grants to support projects such as the leadership associates program, the ESL endorsement courses, and the K–2 literacy project. Partnership school districts contribute an annual fee for operational expenses totaling roughly $10,000. They provide additional contributions through released time for the teachers and administrators, who spend countless hours in committees and other work of CITES.

It has been projected that the regular annual operating budget for CITES will be in the range of $300,000 to $350,000, with about $200,000 going toward the costs of hiring personnel—the executive director, full- and part-time secretarial help, professorships, student assistance, and released time for other participants—and the remainder being used for communications, supplies, travel, and equipment. Additional funding will need to be secured to finance the projects undertaken at the direction of CITES. At the time of this writing, $100,000 has been awarded by the academic vice president as phase I of the funding of CITES, targeted specifically for salaries and benefits for the full-time executive director and secretary. The university vice president has made the permanence and increase of this budget contingent on the following conditions:

1. The formation of strong partnerships between BYU departments, the School of Education, and local schools to improve teacher preparation
2. The admission of as many students who are interested in elementary and secondary teacher preparation as possible
3. The dissemination of learning from research and practice related to improved teacher preparation and student learning through both publication and other outlets that influence the participants in the partnership and the larger national audience
4. The ability to obtain additional external funding from partners in this effort, as well as from external funding agencies
5. The continuation of contributions to the national renewal effort of which CITES is a part[8]

These conditions, as well as the provision of funding by the university, are evidence of the administration's commitment to CITES.

Further evidence of commitment is the administration's approval of major renovations in the building that houses the David O. McKay School of Education in order to provide appropriate facilities for CITES.

Publicity and Recognition

Very little publicity and no formal celebration accompanied the first announcement of CITES. Although there was no conscious decision at the beginning to withhold publicity and limit operation and expectations for CITES to those who have been directly involved, time has shown this to have been a beneficial strategy. Had there been wider interest and enthusiasm for CITES, the proliferation of projects and activities might have been overwhelming. Being largely unheralded for the first two years allowed valuable time for developing organizational and management strategies to handle the growth in activity that occurred.

Now that CITES has become better known, a wider variety of people and projects are involved, and the attitudes and expectations of many will need to be changed. Changing the attitudes that dominate a culture is never an easy task, particularly when large numbers of individuals are involved. Traditionally, university and public school personnel have been more aware of their differences than of their common needs and interests. People who in the past have not been treated with respect remember the difficulties and are constantly testing the rhetoric to see whether the claims that are touted for collaboration are sincere. Size also presents a challenge. BYU graduates over one thousand teacher candidates a year, and the five school districts of BYU-PSP represent over one-third of Utah's school population. The turnover in faculty and administrators of both systems means a continuous campaign to keep people informed and to promote unity in philosophy and perspective. And, of course, individual personalities can frustrate collaboration. It is one thing to affirm the value of collaborative relationships, but quite another to foster the kind of patience and trust that enables people to look past frustrations and mixed messages that may arise between participants in such a system.

Support for an institution like the Center for the Improvement of Teacher Education and Schooling cannot be legislated; it must be won. CITES participants and supporters can only hope that the results of current and future projects will be sufficiently compelling to strengthen the commitment of those already involved in collaborative partnering and to entice others to join in and support opportunities for collaboration.

6

The University of Texas at El Paso

During the academic year 1997–1998, five "graduates" of the Institute for Educational Inquiry's Leadership Program planned and implemented a year-long Institute for Educational Renewal in El Paso, Texas. The institute brought together senior administrators and faculty members from the Colleges of Education, Science, and Liberal Arts at the University of Texas at El Paso (UTEP); public school administrators and teachers from the El Paso area; and members of the El Paso Collaborative for Academic Excellence. During four three-day sessions, this group shared common readings concerning the nature and responsibilities of teacher education, as well as the simultaneous renewal of public schools and programs that prepare teachers. This institute was one of several initiatives designed to bring teacher educators, representatives from the public schools, and faculty from arts and sciences departments of the university together in order to strengthen both teacher education and public school practice simultaneously.

UTEP does not currently have a center of pedagogy. Its College of Education is moving in the direction of such a center, however, as it continues to find ways to bring the participants and stakeholders in teacher education together to combine and coordinate their efforts for the benefit of both the university and the schools.

Because the university serves the needs of a predominantly working-class, minority population in both its student body and the schools in which its graduates will generally teach, this chapter illustrates how needs and tensions unique to such a community can be met through collaborative work. Obstacles and challenges, though in some ways unique to the El Paso situation, have much in common with the obstacles many institutions face as they move from disparate (and sometimes hostile) participants in teacher education, through initial steps in collaboration, eventually to approach the firmly structured collaboration represented by a center of pedagogy.

The Settings

Any teacher education program is a product of and must be responsive to the settings in which it develops. In the case of UTEP, the settings of the El Paso community and the UTEP campus have raised definite and specific needs in teacher education and have generated opposition that has sometimes made it difficult to respond to those needs.

The El Paso Region

The city of El Paso is a bustling urban area of 700,000 people, more than 70 percent of whom are of Mexican descent. Sitting on the Rio Grande River in the westernmost corner of Texas on the borders of Mexico and New Mexico, El Paso has for four hundred years been a major passage for emigrants through the mountains from Mexico to what is now the United States. The city became known as *el paso del norte*, the "passage to the north." Across the river from El Paso sits the Mexican city of Juarez, a city of more than 1.2 million people; the El Paso–Juarez complex represents the largest metropolitan area along the two-thousand-mile U.S.-Mexico border.

Today the city of El Paso reflects the hopes, aspirations, and dreams of its working-class population, but the city and its residents continue to be marked by great need. The region suffers from high levels of poverty, high unemployment, and low educational attainment. El Paso's metropolitan area is the fifth poorest in the United States. Isolated from the rest of Texas, El Paso receives less than its share of state resources. For example, the area along the Texas-Mexico border has 20 percent of the state's population but receives only 10 percent of the state's resources for higher education. In addition, two of its urban school districts (two of the eight largest in Texas) have a long history of severe underfunding. Given these conditions of isolation and poverty, the university, since its inception, has played a central role in meeting the aspirations of the people of the El Paso region. The next closest public university in Texas is more than 250 miles away.

The University

The struggle of teacher education to gain strength, even respectability, at UTEP can be best understood in terms of the university's early history.

UTEP did not originate as a normal school, as did so many other public institutions that prepare large numbers of teachers; it began as the Texas State School of Mines and Metallurgy. Established in 1914 "for the purpose of teaching the scientific knowledge of mining and metallurgy," the School of Mines was founded under the supervision of the regents of the University of Texas. The school was a response to an important regional need. Quite isolated from the rest of Texas, El Paso, in addition to being an important east-west and north-south crossroads and trade route, had by 1900 also become the headquarters for prospectors and miners of the high desert regions of El Paso, northern Mexico, New Mexico, and Arizona. Because El Paso was quickly becoming a center for gold, silver, and, later, copper refining, the School of Mines was needed to prepare mining engineers and geologists. The mines were generating a large population: between 1900 and 1920, El Paso's population grew fourfold, from fifteen thousand to sixty thousand.

Almost from the start there were pressures to expand the narrow technical curriculum of the school to include broader offerings and more varied training. As early as 1917, pressure came from both the El Paso community and the state capital for the School of Mines to consider offering course work that would prepare teachers and grant teaching certificates. The school's first dean, trained as an analytic chemist and mining engineer, held fast to the narrower scope of the school. He wrote to the president of the University of Texas at Austin: "The subject of teachers certificates was mentioned, but was rejected because it was thought that the granting of such certificates would tend to lower the standing of the school and place it on a plain [sic] with the normal schools."[1] Thus from the very beginning there were seeds of a tension that would be a barrier to teacher education at UTEP throughout its development, a tension that has been common to higher education across the nation for most of this century.[2] This tension continues to surface, ebbing and flowing as discrepancies become evident among the state's interests, the community's interests, the varying interests of arts and sciences faculty, and the concerns of College of Education faculty.

By 1917, just three years after the School of Mines started offering courses, El Paso had developed into a thriving community. It was the major center of commerce for hundreds of miles in that part of West Texas, with schools, churches, and a number of important businesses. Because the School of Mines resisted offering a broader curriculum in the arts or engaging in the preparation of teachers, community leaders started an alternative institution, the College of the City of El Paso. The new college was to include a "normal department" headed by the superintendent of city schools. The college's first bulletin specified a full four-year program, with classes to be taught at the newly built El Paso High School.[3]

Both institutions struggled during their early years. In 1920, the College of the City of El Paso was transformed into a junior college for the preparation of teachers, and by 1921 it had 106 students and 16 faculty, all housed on the top floor of El Paso High School. At this time the School of Mines, with 93 students, was feeling the pressure of competition. Finally, in 1927, through a compromise among key community members and legislators, the scope of the College of Mines was enlarged, with the stipulation that any subject would be added to its curriculum if demanded by a minimum of 10 or 12 students.[4] With the need for its existence eliminated by the expansion of the College of Mines, the junior college closed, and several of its faculty members moved to the newly expanded institution.

Soon after preparation of teachers was transferred to the College of Mines, the first professor of education became acting dean of the college, a position in which he had full authority to direct operations of the college, supervised only by the president of the University of Texas and its board of regents. From this position, he was able to create teacher preparation programs. Although reluctant to take advantage of his authority, he nevertheless set out to expand opportunities for teacher training and for a broader curriculum in the arts, within the financial constraints set by the parent university at Austin.

The pressure from the community for teacher certification programs continued to be intense. The superintendent of schools wrote that he had more than three hundred teachers waiting for courses at the college, preferably courses taught in the evening.[5] By 1930 the population of El Paso had reached 100,000, and enrollment at the college had swelled to over 600. The college, with its expanded curriculum in education and the arts, was coming into its own. By 1931 a full-fledged bachelor of arts degree was offered, in addition to the bachelor of science degree in mining engineering. The work of training teachers was once again on a firm footing. A collection of courses leading to the teaching certificate finally developed into an education major in 1936.

This description of the origins of teacher preparation at UTEP is consistent with the history and plight of teacher education at colleges and universities across the country. Regardless of their origins as normal schools, research universities, liberal arts colleges, regional universities, or specialized single-purpose institutions (like the College of Mines), almost all of these institutions have experienced a great deal of dissonance and uncertainty about teacher preparation programs. As John Goodlad points out in *Teachers for Our Nation's Schools*, this is true even in institutions that began as normal schools, founded specifically for the training of teachers. As they have expanded and grown in prominence over the years, many have gradually diminished the role of teacher preparation.[6] This diminution has often occurred despite intense pressures from communities and the education profession, and despite the fact that these institutions depend heavily on prospective teachers for their increasing enrollments and tuition dollars.

The diminution of teacher preparation at the College of Mines followed the same pattern. Although the College of Arts and Sciences at UTEP had its beginning with the demands from the community and from school professionals for the training of teachers, faculty who were hired to staff the arts and sciences departments quickly began to distance themselves from teacher preparation. As Charles Silberman notes, they thought such work was below them: "With familiar academic hauteur, they regarded schooling (especially schooling for the masses) as a subject not worthy of the concern of genuine (and gentlemanly) scholars."[7] Even within colleges and schools of education, Goodlad suggests, those who could more readily identify themselves with a traditional arts or sciences discipline (especially psychology) often attempted to distance themselves from their colleagues whose primary work was the preparation of teachers.[8] This has been and continues to be a significant dilemma for the profession of education. For most of its history, teacher preparation in El Paso has experienced this attitude and behavior.

From Hostility to Collaboration

The years following the establishment of a department and a major in education in the 1930s were marked by fairly continual growth of the teacher education programs, paralleling the overall growth of the

El Paso community and the college. By 1960, the college had more than five thousand students, nearly eight hundred of them preparing to become teachers. Another hundred were doing graduate work in education. In 1967, the College of Arts and Sciences was divided into four colleges: Business Administration, Education, Liberal Arts, and Science. In 1970 a new nine-story education building opened. In the decade between 1967 and 1977, the number of full-time faculty in the new College of Education grew from nineteen to forty-two, and by the end of that span of years there were approximately two thousand students preparing to become teachers.

Enrollments, facilities, and even national recognition were coming to the teacher preparation program at El Paso. However, this did not result in either the respect from the other programs or the satisfaction that the teacher education faculty sought. Rapid growth, dissension within the college, and insufficient support from the academic community and the state threatened to destroy the teacher education program. Finally, a movement toward collaboration became the turning point in bringing the program back to a course of positive development.

Problems and Crises

By 1970 nearly one-third of all degrees awarded by the university were bachelor of science degrees in education, and the increased quality of the teacher preparation programs was recognized by the National Council for Accreditation of Teacher Education (NCATE) with its accreditation of UTEP's College of Education in 1975. But all was not as well as it should have been in the 1970s and 1980s. It is difficult to determine what went wrong—perhaps several things at once.

Rapid growth itself may have been part of the problem. The College of Education had grown large enough to have its share of internal bickering and leadership problems. For example, in 1974 a young member of the faculty who had been a UTEP student was appointed by the president as dean of the College of Education, to the consternation of some other members of the faculty. She was the first female, the first Hispanic, and the first graduate of UTEP to be named dean of a college. She remained dean for six years, the longest tenure in recent history, and she had some notable accomplishments during her deanship, especially in the areas of NCATE accreditation, bilingual education, and multicultural education. However, a good part of her tenure was marked by faculty dissension, resentment, and bickering. Afterward there were several major shifts in deanships in the college and major changes in the positions of president and vice president of the university as well.

In the early 1980s, stability slowly began to return to the College of Education: A new dean was recruited after several interim deans, and the academic work of the faculty and mission of the college were redefined. A renewed emphasis was placed on scholarly productivity, and a new promotion and tenure system was developed. In the spring of 1987, however, the state legislature dropped a bombshell on the college, passing Senate Bill 994. This legislation, which went into effect in 1991, abolished the education major in public colleges and universities in Texas and capped the maximum hours in education that a student could take as part of teacher certification. Thus, students preparing to become elementary teachers would have to take most of their course work in the colleges of arts and sciences, with no more than eighteen semester hours in education courses. Students preparing to become high school teachers would have to major in the discipline that they planned to teach in high school—for example, students planning to be high school math teachers would have to earn a degree in mathematics, and prospective English teachers a degree in English.

It has been suggested that this bill was part of the legislative backlash against the schools, teachers, and, by extension, programs that prepare teachers that began with the publication of *A Nation at Risk* in 1983.[9] That caustic critique of the schools fed an already declining public confidence in the public schools and colleges of education that continues nearly unabated to this day.[10] The logic behind Senate Bill 994 may have been that if students were not learning at the appropriate level, it was the fault of the teachers. And, by extension, if teachers were not successful, it was because they were ill prepared because of taking too many courses in education and not enough in the traditional academic disciplines. This logic also fed the growing disdain toward and criticism of the faculty and courses of the College of Education by some arts and sciences faculty members at UTEP.

Courses and semester credit hour production are the lifeblood of universities, and suddenly abolishing the education major had a devastating effect on the morale of the faculty of the College of Education. As a further blow, the education faculty now had to work with their scornful colleagues in the arts and sciences to fashion a new degree and formulate a revised program of studies for those preparing to become elementary and middle school teachers. The compromise was a new degree, bachelor of interdisciplinary studies, 85 percent of which was composed of courses from the arts and sciences. Only at the junior and senior levels would students take the maximum eighteen hours of courses in education. Similar solutions and compromises were worked out in the many teacher preparation institutions across Texas. Acrimony from the debates and forced compromises of the late 1980s continues among some faculty to this day, and this unfortunate legacy has been a major barrier to overcome in the more recent and successful efforts to launch university-wide efforts to improve the preparation of teachers.

In the College of Education, a sort of malaise set in among the faculty, and although the college survived the bomb, many felt that it was on the decline, as its central purpose for existence had been severely challenged. With the loss of the education major and many of the courses that had supported faculty, the college's faculty was diminished, and there was a sense, both internally and externally, that the college was languishing. Many faculty members believed that senior administrators of the university were unhappy with the leaders of the College of Education and did not seem to care very much about the future of the college. Unfortunately, there was little support from the community. Many professional educators in the community—most of them graduates of the college—had become alienated from it and its work. There were some discussions among senior administrators about whether a College of Education was even needed.

The Beginning of Renewal

Although the College of Education was experiencing discouragement and rejection, UTEP overall was enjoying growth and affirmation at this time. This growth of the larger unit, coupled with the importance of teacher preparation in the geographic area, brought efforts at renewal to teacher educators in spite of their recent setbacks.

The opening of the 1990s brought a new sense of vitality to the UTEP campus. Enrollments were growing rapidly after a momentary decline in 1986, and energetic and dynamic Diana Natalicio was in the third year of her presidency. Sponsored project activity and other forms of external funding were increasing rapidly, especially in the College of Engineering and the College of Science. The percentage of Hispanic students enrolled at the university had long surpassed 50 percent, and the president had the vision and insight to turn that phenomenon into an advantage. Capitalizing on its status as the largest Hispanic-majority university in the continental United States, with a long history of producing outstanding students in science and engineering, the president led a highly successful effort to bring large institutional grants to UTEP. Between 1992 and 1996, for example, sponsored-project activity at the university increased from $16 million to $33 million. This additional support improved the quality of life for everyone—faculty members, students, and the El Paso community. First in the Colleges of Engineering and Science, and then across the other colleges, a new sense of identity and efficacy began to emerge at UTEP. As the research and sponsored-project activity increased, more outstanding faculty members were attracted, and one by one each of the colleges was renewed.

In education, the real effort at renewal began in 1992. The College of Education was beginning to recover from the malaise of the 1980s, large numbers of teachers were still graduating, and the decline in the number of faculty had leveled off. But the decline in faculty numbers had produced unrealistic demands for those who remained. The college was graduating five hundred new teachers and granting more than one hundred graduate degrees per year with fewer than thirty full-time faculty. Nevertheless, there were beginning to be signs of a turnaround.

In 1992, the university president directed her attention to teacher education. She had led the university in redefining its mission and goals, focusing on the objective of becoming one of the best regional comprehensive universities in the United States, one intimately tied to and serving the community around it. A realistic goal for UTEP was to address the major needs of the community: providing a first-rate college education for the young people in the region and serving the community by providing it with the professional and intellectual expertise that it so desperately needed. It was abundantly clear that both of those major needs depended on improving the life chances of the mostly Hispanic youngsters in El Paso through their success in school. Good teachers were central to this task; something had to be done in education.

Knowing that the College of Education was not yet prepared for the extent of renewal she had in mind, the president herself brought together in early 1992 the key stakeholders in the educational community of El Paso: the superintendents of the three largest school districts, the president of the community college, the heads of the two chambers of commerce, the mayor and the county judge, and the lead organizer of the most active and effective grassroots community organization in the region. Under her leadership, with the direction of a very able and experienced executive director who had done similar work in California, the El Paso Collaborative for

Academic Excellence was launched. This initiative was to be a community-wide systemic reform effort aimed at improving the academic achievement of all young people in El Paso, from preschool through the undergraduate years. The initial effort would focus on working to improve the teaching force in the schools.

The collaborative, which met regularly with essentially the same participants, had a major impact in raising the achievement of the 130,000 P–12 students in El Paso. It has been cited in several national sources for making El Paso, with its data-driven systemic reform efforts, a bright spot among urban districts.[11] It has attracted millions of dollars to bring state-of-the-art expertise and continuous professional development to the teachers and schools of El Paso and has gained long-term support from the National Science Foundation, The Pew Charitable Trusts, and several other foundations, as well as the state of Texas.

The El Paso Collaborative has become the umbrella under which other reform efforts have been launched. In this role, it has kept a variety of reform groups focused on the same goal: improving the academic achievement of all students in El Paso. One of its most recent products is a set of academic standards in seven areas at the fourth-, eighth-, and twelfth-grade levels. Based on national standards where available, this selection of standards took two years to develop, with the participation of hundreds of teachers, university professors, and community members. They have been accepted by the school boards of the districts, and posters with these standards for academic achievement (in English and Spanish) now hang in almost every classroom in El Paso. After being launched by the governor in a special visit to El Paso in 1996, the standards are being implemented into the curriculum to help improve all aspects of teaching and learning in the schools.

Renewal in Teacher Training

Shortly after the El Paso Collaborative was established, UTEP's president turned her attention to the College of Education, sensing that the renewal of teacher training in the university was essential to the success of the effort to reform teaching in the schools. In the late spring of 1992, she attended a retreat of the College of Education faculty, bringing with her the director of the El Paso Collaborative. They outlined some of the goals of the Collaborative, suggesting that there was an important role to be played by the college. In preparation for the retreat, the college faculty had read some of John Goodlad's work and were impressed by the possibilities that he outlined. During the retreat, they focused on the need for improvement, including the importance of developing stronger ties to the education profession and to the schools in the region. At the conclusion of the retreat, the faculty committed itself to a process of revamping the college into a "professional school," with better collaboration with and ties to the public schools.

The renewal effort began soon after the retreat, with strong support from the president. In her September 1992 convocation address to the faculty and staff, the president called attention to UTEP's necessary commitment to the preparation of educators. She spoke first of the El Paso Collaborative:

> The importance of this systemic approach to school reform has been recognized by the American Association of Higher Education, which has selected the El Paso Collaborative as one of ten sites nationally to receive funding from The Pew Charitable Trusts, and by the Coca-Cola Foundation, which has recently awarded it $150,000 to carry out its important work. Encouraged by such high-level recognition and supported by the National Science Foundation through the Comprehensive Regional Center for Minorities, the Collaborative is well on its way to laying the foundation for new ways of thinking about precollegiate education and UTEP's role in enhancing it. Highly successful institutes were conducted this past summer for hundreds of teachers, counselors, principals,

and other administrators from the Ysleta, Socorro, and El Paso school districts, and a broad range of follow-up activities are planned for this academic year.

She then turned her attention to the role of the College of Education in collaboration with the schools:

A critical element in the Collaborative's development will be UTEP's commitment to enhance preservice teacher preparation. New leadership in the College of Education and an invitation to UTEP to be a participant in the highly regarded National Network for Educational Renewal will advance this agenda significantly, but it is increasingly clear that responsibility for teacher preparation does not rest solely with the College of Education. When we consider the fact that 86 percent of UTEP's students are products of El Paso County schools and an estimated 80 percent of the teachers in those schools hold degrees from this university, it is clear that in this closed loop we all have a stake in preparing the best teachers who will, in turn, raise the expectation and achievement levels of our future students. If we would like to be able to raise UTEP's admission requirements by the year 2001 to include specified units of mathematics, science, English, social studies, foreign languages, and the like, we must commit ourselves—all of us—to partner with our colleagues in the public schools in this region to enhance their capacity to provide the strong precollegiate preparation we seek. To sit back, take no action, and complain about the underpreparation of new generations of students is not in our self-interest and certainly not likely to lead this region toward academic excellence.[12]

At the time that the president gave her address in September, the College of Education faculty were already reading materials by

Goodlad and his colleagues, attending meetings, and discussing the possibility of applying for membership in the National Network for Educational Renewal (NNER). The new dean of the college had already spent a week at the Institute for Educational Inquiry in Seattle as a Leadership Associate during August, and he had returned enthusiastic about the possibilities. The university submitted a twelve-page application to join the NNER in October, and in November 1992 was accepted as a member.

Membership and participation in the NNER have been instrumental in providing a framework for the renewal agenda of the College of Education at UTEP. Whether dealing with the hiring of new faculty, establishing collaborative relationships with partnership schools, designing the new teacher preparation program, or seeking new resources and grants, the college has been guided by one central question: Will this move advance the simultaneous renewal of schooling and teacher preparation? Upholding values absolutely compatible with those of the El Paso Collaborative, the college was always cognizant of the collaborative's bottom line: Will this effort contribute to the improvement of academic achievement and to the well-being of all youngsters in the El Paso region?

Antecedents for a Center of Pedagogy

UTEP's College of Education has benefited from its association with the NNER and from the examples of centers of pedagogy currently in operation at Montclair State University and Brigham Young University (BYU). UTEP does not have a center of pedagogy at this time, but recent developments are opening up possibilities and moving the College of Education in this general direction.

Preparation and Conversation

Since joining the NNER in late 1992, the El Paso setting has sent five individuals to participate in the year-long Leadership Associates Program of the Institute for Educational Inquiry that Goodlad and his colleagues have developed in Seattle. Their participation has been important in building a critical mass of individuals who are prepared to participate in pursuing a change agenda in teacher preparation. These five individuals—the dean of the College of Education, an assistant dean, a key senior faculty member in teacher education, a principal of a vital partner school, and a central player in the El Paso Collaborative for Academic Excellence—were chosen for their strategic roles in the reform effort and their ability to extend the conversation about reform to other setting participants. Sharing a set of common assumptions and supporting Goodlad's nineteen postulates,[13] they have helped to keep the renewal agenda moving.

The Leadership Associates have also been key contributors to a series of important conversations among university faculty and public school colleagues about the university's mission of preparing teachers. These conversations continue, necessarily, at several levels: in the El Paso Collaborative among the educational, civic, and business leaders of the community; between university faculty members, helping to draw new faculty members into the discussion of the university's responsibility in preparing teachers; and between university faculty and public school teachers about their common interests and responsibilities for the learning of young people. Conversations are also taking place between faculty and administrators across colleges that often seem to be at cross-purposes. Although some of the conversations are not initially easy, it is out of these dialogues that opportunities arise to work together and keep the agenda going.

A New Teacher Preparation Program

Conversations among the faculty in teacher education and with public school teaching colleagues led to a complete revamping of the teacher preparation program. Drawing on the experience of other institutions, current research on teacher preparation, and the orientation and values central to the nineteen postulates of the NNER, the College of Education faculty set out with both arts and sciences faculty and public school partners to create a new teacher preparation program.

The resulting program is field based, sending student interns to partnership schools for far longer periods of time than the traditional twelve weeks of student teaching. Influenced by the medical school model, the program arranges for students to take their campus classes in cohorts of thirty students, after which they are sent (still in cohorts) to approximately twenty partnership schools to engage in their "clinical practice," under the joint supervision of university professors and mentor clinical faculty in the schools. In the traditional program, students were sent out singly and in pairs to more than a hundred schools for their twelve weeks of student teaching. In the new program, students extend their clinical internships throughout their senior year. During these final two semesters at college, a student typically spends a day or two per week at the university completing the professional education course work and two or three days at the partnership school, going back and forth as a means to bridge theory and practice. The partnership schools have been chosen carefully from the seventy schools that had already made a commitment to renewal through their ongoing participation in the systemic reform effort of the El Paso Collaborative.

With a large grant from the state of Texas to restructure the teacher preparation program in collaboration with public school partners, the college faculty began to put the new program in place in 1993. The grant created the Center for Professional Development and Technology, and it provided some resources in technology and professional development to each of the partnership schools. The college gave itself three years to make the complete transition from the traditional program to the new, and for the three transition years between 1993 and 1996 it operated both programs, allowing students who were already in the old program to choose and requiring new students to enroll in the new program. The work involved intense collaboration, and the lives of all participants changed significantly. The partnership schools were now hosting as many as twenty to thirty interns at a time and taking on greater responsibility for their professional development than they had under the traditional format. University faculty who taught in the program were scheduled to teach in blocks and expected to follow their students into the schools for visits. The interns were now block scheduled and required to spend many daytime hours in the public schools; in contrast, the traditional program, with its limited field-work, could be completed almost entirely in the evening. Students also took their common course work in cohorts, and many team activities were structured into the experience. This kind of scheduling played havoc with outside jobs and family obligations. Students, faculty, and public school personnel were required to put forth considerable effort and to make personal sacrifices along the way.

With the many changes and sacrifices required, the success of this venture would have been highly unlikely if participants had not shared a common vision; respect for each other's experience, constraints, and expertise; and a strong commitment to ongoing discussion and dialogue. The program changes involved a good deal of trust and faith in colleagues, as well as in the leadership of the university and the schools. All of the stakeholders, including the students, had important roles to play; all were listened to carefully in the refining and fine-tuning of the program.

By the end of 1996 the new program was completely in place, and the old one no longer existed. Reports from teachers and principals about the graduates of the new program have generally been quite positive, especially concerning the graduates' knowledge of educational innovations and their greater familiarity with the schools. Many people in the schools seem to be changing their image of the university, considering it an interested and respectful partner in a common endeavor, rather than holding the traditional stereotypical view of a one-way flow of expertise (and condescension) from the university to the public schools. Central to this respectful relationship between the public schools and the university has been the establishment of a new governance structure, the Teacher Center

Council, which, although chaired by the dean of the College of Education, has far more representation of teachers and partner school principals than it does representatives of the university faculty.

Administrative and Cross-Campus Support

Perhaps the most difficult conversation is the one that must take place between faculty of the College of Education and faculty in the arts and sciences, because of the long history of poor relationships between faculty in these areas. In addition to holding elitist views about their disciplines compared with the field of education, arts and sciences faculty members in universities often feel little or no responsibility for the preparation of teachers. It is not uncommon for cross-campus faculty to place the total responsibility for training teachers on college of education faculty and then to blame them for the poor job that they are doing. For their part, faculty members from education often see arts and sciences faculty as ivory tower elitists with no interest in addressing real-world problems. The state of Texas and the University of Texas at El Paso have not been exceptions to this pattern.

From the beginning of the UTEP renewal effort, it was clear that if the reform was to be successful, personnel from the entire university had to be involved. Support had first to be secured from the president of the university and then from deans and faculty members in the arts and sciences. Support from all was essential if the university culture was to change sufficiently to view the responsibility for teacher preparation as university-wide, not just the purview of the College of Education. Crucial support from the president was easiest to gain, as is evident in her 1992 State of the University address, already quoted in this chapter. She embraced the renewal agenda and encouraged the dean of education to move forward with her support. Working with the dean of the College of Science, the president created three new science educator faculty positions in that college. This was the first time that faculty from the College of Science had been recruited for the specific purpose of preparing math and science teachers. Without this kind of administrative and cross-campus support, success in any major university reform effort is unlikely.[14]

Even with this kind of support, the task of engaging arts and sciences administrators and faculty in teacher preparation is daunting. In addition to support from the president, the reform effort at UTEP has benefited greatly from taking advantage of fortuitous events and structured opportunities to engage others in conversations about change. Three such opportunities at UTEP have advanced the agenda by engaging faculty from the arts and sciences.

The first opportunity occurred in 1993, when faculty members in the College of Education and those in the College of Science decided to respond to an initiative from the National Science Foundation (NSF) to fund Collaboratives for Excellence in Teacher Preparation in the areas of mathematics and science. In one of the initial conversations, the chair of the mathematics department and the dean of education had their first encounter. The outcome was that the math chair recognized his department's responsibility in the preparation of teachers, and both the math chair and the dean realized the necessity of continuing to work together toward the common goal of graduating better teachers. The conversation continued and led to a major grant proposal to NSF, which was funded after two years of conversation and collaboration. With the dean of the College of Education and the dean of the College of Science as co-principal investigators, the grant provided $5 million of funding over five years to bring together faculty from the Colleges of Science and Education, as well as the local community college, to improve the preservice preparation of math and science teachers. Now more than thirty college faculty are engaged in an ongoing conversation about how to improve mathematics and science teaching, and they are given ample opportunity and resources to revise their courses, work on their pedagogy, do research on their innovations, and attend conferences that contribute to their scholarly and teaching competence. The benefits of the grant are extended to a comparable number of public school teachers and informal science site directors, who provide their perspectives and expertise as teachers of young children. As a result, math and science course work required of all elementary teachers has been significantly increased, and all of the mathematics and science courses have been revised to respond better to the needs of the profession.

The second opportunity for collaboration between education and arts and sciences faculty involved faculty members from the College of Liberal Arts. Participating with three other institutions under a small grant from the Fund for the Improvement of Postsecondary Education (FIPSE), a small group of faculty members from liberal arts has been exploring the faculty reward structure for liberal arts faculty members who involve themselves in teacher preparation. First initiated in 1995 through the dean of the College of Education, the Faculty Rewards Project has brought liberal arts faculty into a conversation about teacher preparation through the perspectives of their disciplinary backgrounds and the culture of their college. The FIPSE grant provided funding and a structured opportunity to sustain an extended conversation between College of Education and liberal arts faculty. With strong support from the dean of the College of Liberal Arts, a small group explored the implications of their own involvement as individual faculty members with teacher preparation and also the involvement of their departments.

The third opportunity to engage arts and sciences faculty and administrators in a structured conversation about teacher preparation was the year-long Institute for Educational Renewal held during the academic year 1997–1998, funded by a DeWitt Wallace–Reader's Digest Fund Incentive Award. The institute brought together senior administrators and faculty members from three colleges (Education, Science, and Liberal Arts), public school administrators, and members of the El Paso Collaborative for Academic Excellence. Among the participants were five deans, as well as department chairs, area superintendents of schools, elementary and secondary school principals, and the director of the El Paso Collaborative. During the year, these individuals participated in four three-day retreats, during which they shared reactions to common readings on such topics as the role of schools and universities in a democracy, the preparation of teachers, the moral responsibility of teachers, the problems of access to knowledge, and the need for simultaneous renewal of the public schools and programs that prepare teachers. The institute provided a structured opportunity for extended conversation and reflection among concerned individuals across the boundaries of colleges, departments, the university, and the public schools. In fact, the boundaries themselves were a topic of conversation.

This institute replicated relevant aspects of the Seattle model but was very sensitive to the context and processes of educational change in the El Paso setting. The goal was to extend the conversation and move the simultaneous renewal agenda forward, particularly into the engagement of arts and sciences faculty members. In this regard, the institute was outstanding, and it has been critical in moving the El Paso setting toward the development of a center of pedagogy.

Participants in the College of Education, the El Paso Collaborative for Academic Excellence, and a number of arts and sciences departments across the university are developing conditions that will enable a center of pedagogy to be formed in the future. Like Montclair State University and Brigham Young University, El Paso is concerned with the simultaneous renewal of the public schools and the programs that prepare educators; decisions concerning teacher education are made on the basis of whether they contribute to the renewal agenda. El Paso looks forward to future development.

Part III

Developing Successful
Centers of Pedagogy

The concept of a center of pedagogy emerged through the controversy and turmoil of educational reform: the criticism of schools, denunciation of colleges and schools of education, and alienation of various participants in the education enterprise. The concept evolved as colleges of education and public schools began to recognize their interdependence and to form partnerships to renew both simultaneously. Gradually these partnerships became more complex. The center of pedagogy has been refined as a concept and introduced as a practice as partnerships have recognized the importance of uniting three partners—the faculties of education, the arts and sciences, and the schools—in preparing teachers and in designing and providing education for the schools. For maximum effectiveness of programs, these three groups must coordinate their efforts consistent with a common vision and mutually beneficial goals. The center of pedagogy is a structure with the potential to attain this coordination.

Several school-university partnerships and consortia in different areas of the United States are implementing or working toward centers of pedagogy. Among them are Montclair State University, with its Center of Pedagogy; Brigham Young University, with its Center for the Improvement of Teacher Education and Schooling (CITES); and the University of Texas at El Paso, with a collaborative that has many of the characteristics of a center of pedagogy and seems to be moving toward establishing one. These three settings—though varied in location, needs, interests, governance, administrative support, personnel, reward systems, and finance—have underlying similarities that offer insights to any institution recognizing a need for and working in the direction of a center of pedagogy as a coordinating structure.

No significant experience is complete without reflection. In the strengths and weaknesses, the steps and missteps, and the ups and downs experienced by centers of pedagogy are lessons applicable to participants in many different phases and types of educational improvement. The following two chapters reflect on the experiences of the three centers and extend the principles to additional centers throughout the country. The intent is to increase the applicability of the experiences of centers of pedagogy to a variety of settings on a national scale.

Chapter Seven focuses on the three case studies in Part Two, drawing out some of the common aspects of their experiences. Despite their surface differences, the three partnerships were founded on some goals and beliefs common to their tripartite members and surprisingly similar among the three institutions. Conceptions of collaboration and leadership and goals for the coordinating units also have similarities that provide instruction and insight. Items such as reward systems, governance structures, and finance provide some striking contrasts that demonstrate differing ways in which common needs can be met successfully. This chapter distills principles and asks questions.

Chapter Eight generalizes some of the conclusions of Chapter Seven, applying them to other centers, developing centers, and anticipated centers in different sites both inside and outside the National Network for Educational Renewal. A questionnaire was sent to a wide variety of institutions with teacher preparation programs, asking questions to discern their familiarity with the concept of centers of pedagogy, their implementation or prospective implementation of such a center, the nature of tripartite participation in their partnerships, and specific aspects of their coordinating structures, such as shared vision, reward systems, and finance. The results of that study are reported, and descriptions of a number of structures that implement all or some of the aspects of centers of pedagogy are presented. The chapter concludes with suggested principles for assessing a center of pedagogy, along with specific standards and indicators for this assessment.

7

Crosscutting Themes
Goals, Principles, and Obstacles

Moving a school-university partnership toward the development of a center of pedagogy is complex and difficult. In every case, this development takes place under local conditions and through strategies that are unique to the individual partnership and that become major factors in the implementation of the center. Montclair State University, Brigham Young University (BYU), and the University of Texas at El Paso (UTEP) are very different institutions in terms of their size, mission, and Carnegie classification status. They also differ widely in the academic and social contexts in which their partnerships have developed. Generalizations gleaned from the three case studies are limited by the fact that they are, after all, only three case studies with little that is common among the settings. Yet what they do have in common is that all three set out on a renewal agenda with similar goals, guided by a set of shared principles. And all three faced similar obstacles along their separate paths toward the development of centers of pedagogy. With these common characteristics, some analysis can be made and some conclusions drawn from the case studies to inform other institutions that might be considering the development of similar structures.

The Center of Pedagogy as a Response to Need

Common among the obstacles that Montclair State University, BYU, and UTEP faced in their attempts to establish effective collaborative teacher education programs have been misunder-standing and lack of respect from a number of groups whose support is vital to significant renewal of teacher education and schooling. For all three, the movement toward or eventual development of a center of pedagogy has been a series of attempts to counter tradi-tional separation, criticism, and misunderstanding.

Barriers to Collaborative Educational Renewal

In all three cases, the university has had to overcome long-standing antagonisms between colleges of education and colleges of arts and sciences. This enmity has been common in universities for most of this century, and the conflict has been a substantial barrier to efforts to focus the full resources of the university on the preparation of teachers. This antagonism has existed even at universities, like Montclair and BYU, that began as normal schools. In addition to the loss of respect across the colleges, many former normal school administrations lost sight over time of their original founding mis-sions as the universities became larger and more comprehensive in-stitutions. The adversarial positions of education faculty and their arts and sciences colleagues, along with the failure of administra-tions to provide adequate support for teacher preparation, have re-sulted in persistent and well-documented failure to collaborate across colleges in order to share fully the responsibility for the prepa-ration of teachers. It is this failure that has led to the necessity for new organizational structures such as the center of pedagogy.

In addition to this lack of an adequate organizational response to the complex problem of the education of teachers, collaboration is handicapped by a pervasive disrespect, both within and outside universities, for the work of preparing teachers. This disrespect is apparent in the common conception of arts and sciences faculty that all that prospective teachers need is a strong education in the disciplines (content) and that pedagogy—whatever it is—will take care of itself. In this schema, course work in colleges of education is often seen as devoid of a real knowledge base. This view was recently voiced by the director of a national organization of arts and sciences deans who, in a presentation to education deans, said that arts and sciences faculty are concerned with the *education* of students, while education faculty are concerned with the *training* of students. Unfortunately, faculty members in colleges of education sometimes contribute to this view when they fail to ground their work on the results of research and neglect to make a strong enough case that the investigation of teaching and learning—pedagogy— is on a par with work in the traditional disciplines.

This disrespect for the preparation that colleges of education provide is also common outside the university. Both the teaching profession and state legislatures across the nation have been critical of teacher preparation and the colleges of education. Surveys of practicing teachers conducted by both Diana Rigden and Public Agenda found that teachers held negative views of their own preparation programs.[1] Strong and continual public denunciation of teacher preparation programs is a serious barrier to the success of new forms of collaboration, especially those represented by centers of pedagogy. There is far more potential for success in an organizational structure that incorporates allies from both the public schools and the arts and sciences, bringing the resources of all three groups to the complex task of teacher preparation. Three other groups of stakeholders—state policymakers, parents, and community members—are also crucial to keeping renewal on track. In examining the decade of reform represented by the one hundred research universities of the Holmes Group, Michael Fullan and his colleagues have pointed out that the absence of these two vital constituencies has contributed to the stalling of reform.[2]

Another barrier that needs to be overcome in moving toward centers of pedagogy is the perception that teacher preparation is or ought to be a relatively simple matter. It is difficult to find another profession in which actual complexity is so underplayed. The complexity increases as teachers must be prepared for increasingly diverse and needy sets of learners, often in urban settings that are marked by serious social as well as academic difficulties. Michael Fullan and Matthew Miles have said that one of the fundamental reasons for the failure of educational reform has been the failure of reformers to acknowledge the complexity of the educational systems that they are trying to reform:

> Education *is* a complex system, and its reform is even more complex. Even if one considers only seemingly simple, first-order changes, the number of components and their interrelationships are staggering: curriculum and instruction, school organization, student services, community involvement, teacher inservice training, assessment, reporting, and evaluation. Deeper, second-order changes in school cultures, teacher/student relationships, and values and expectations of the system are all the more daunting.
>
> Furthermore, higher-order educational goals for all students require knowledge and abilities that we have never demonstrated. In many cases, we simply don't know how to proceed; solutions have yet to be developed.[3]

Despite this complexity of both the educational enterprise and its reform, state legislatures, the general public, and even the large number of stakeholders involved in either preparing or receiving new teachers are likely either to demand a quick fix or to pronounce a reform effort a failure before it has the time or resources to be fully implemented.

The Concept of and Setting for a Center of Pedagogy

The renewal agendas in the three settings described in the case studies in Part Two have been guided by a common vision of what a center of pedagogy entails. John Goodlad describes that common vision in the opening chapter of his book *Educational Renewal*:

A center of pedagogy is both a concept and a setting. As a concept, it brings together simultaneously and inte- gratively the commonly scattered pieces of the teacher education enterprise and embeds them in reflective at- tention to the art and science of teaching. . . . The term *center of pedagogy* connotes for me an inquiring setting for the education of educators that embraces schools and universities. . . .

How humans learn and how they can best be taught are subjects of great importance and profound complex- ity. For teacher education programs not to be connected with ongoing inquiry into these domains is to guarantee their mediocrity and inadequacy. The best assurance of this connection is for teacher education to be conducted in centers of inquiry focused on this learning and teach- ing—that is, in centers of pedagogy where the art and science of teaching are brought to bear on the education of educators and where the *whole* is the subject of con- tinuous inquiry. Only then will professional programs avoid stagnation and be renewed. In concept, then, a center of pedagogy is both systemic and dynamic. It en- visions faculty members representing the necessary com- ponents of coherent teacher education programs coming together in informed dialogue to sustain renewal—their own and their programs'. In so doing, they demonstrate to their students (and ideally involve them in) the very processes of reflective renewal desired in individual teachers and schools.[4]

To what extent have the three settings described in the previ- ous chapters approximated this ideal? To what extent does each set- ting demonstrate a clear sense of shared mission and responsibility, by tripartite collaboration and by sustained inquiry into teaching and learning? What can be learned from each of these settings? What common features are to be found throughout the different phases of their development?

Components Common to Operating and Developing Centers

Four main components are common to all three of the settings explored in Part Two: (1) development of a shared mission and responsibility common to the tripartite partnership, (2) achievement of levels of trust among the stakeholders, (3) development of a common decision-making or governance structure, and (4) dedication of significant funding for building collaboration and implementing centers of pedagogy. Each of these characteristics corresponds to one or more of the nineteen postulates, or sustaining conditions for simultaneous renewal, advanced by Goodlad and embraced by the National Network for Educational Renewal (NNER).

Shared Mission and Responsibility

Clearly the participants at Montclair State University, BYU, and UTEP have spent years developing a shared mission and establishing shared responsibility for the preparation of educators. The leaders at all of the settings have been thoughtful and deliberate in building a critical mass of strategically placed individuals with a common vision of the necessity of simultaneous renewal.

Central in the formation of this critical mass for change has been the Leadership Associates Program of the Institute for Educational Inquiry (IEI) in Seattle. From 1992 to 1998, all three of the institutions sent professors, university administrators, and public school teachers and administrators to participate in the year-long program of discussion and analysis of educational renewal. Leadership Associates have returned to their settings and formed teams that are prepared with a common vision and sense of moral purpose to guide them as change agents. In all three cases, these teams have initiated leadership programs in their own settings, modeled closely after the IEI's program, and have engaged many others in extended conversations about necessary change and educational renewal. Leadership Associates have also returned from their Seattle experience with close connections to a set of like-minded colleagues in the sixteen settings that compose the NNER.

Building this critical mass of dedicated and well-informed individuals has been significant in the forward movement of the renewal agenda at each setting. The important translation of theory and moral purpose to a practical agenda for change may be the important difference that distinguishes the NNER strategy from that of other reform efforts. Fullan and his colleagues point out that a serious shortcoming of the first ten years of the Holmes Group's reform effort has been its failure to "fulfill its considerable potential because it failed to pursue its own action agenda in any depth."[5]

Trust Among the Partners

The slow and deliberate expansion of the renewal conversation in each setting has gradually built trust among the stakeholders. Montclair State, BYU, and UTEP have all been working at this process of building trust among the stakeholders since at least 1991. Building trust has been difficult because of the complexity of P–16 education in each setting, with its distinct subcultures, modes of discourse, traditional enmity, and seemingly different goals. But the Leadership Associates have served as cultural brokers and border-crossers between the schools, the colleges of education, and the colleges of arts and sciences. These Associates have functioned as cultural workers and interpreters between those who in the past have had little to say to one another, enabling them to communicate effectively as they undertake common tasks.

Decision Making and Governance

Montclair State, BYU, and UTEP have all created decision-making and governance structures suitable to their own local conditions and existing organizational contexts. BYU and Montclair now have semiautonomous centers of pedagogy marked by new organizational structures, with separate directors and appropriate reporting procedures. BYU's Center for the Improvement of Teacher Education and Schooling (CITES) and Montclair's Center of Pedagogy are among the first such centers in the nation. The third setting, at UTEP, does not yet have a formal center, but its El Paso Collaborative for Academic Excellence functions as a reform umbrella that provides many of the enabling conditions for a center.

All three of these settings have decision-making or governance structures that have evolved out of long-standing school-university partnerships. Like many other such collaboratives across the country, these partnerships did not initially include the arts and sciences as vital members. CITES has evolved out of a very long-standing school-university partnership, which has had both a governing board and a management team. The governing board is composed of the superintendents of the school districts in the partnership, the academic vice president of the university, and the dean of the School of Education. The management team is headed by the dean of the School of Education as CITES director, with three associate directors—one each from the public schools, the School of Education, and the arts and sciences.

Montclair's Center of Pedagogy also evolved out of an enduring school-university partnership, the New Jersey Network for Educational Renewal. The Center of Pedagogy has an autonomous director, who reports to an appointed advisory board composed of faculty from education, the arts and sciences, and the schools, as well as the dean of the College of Education and Human Services and the dean of the College of Science and Mathematics. The first director held a faculty position in the College of Education and Human Services, although she could have held a position in either the arts and sciences or the public schools. The chair of the advisory board rotates with each meeting among the tripartite membership. The board meets quarterly to set policy and to oversee the operation of the Center of Pedagogy.

Although Montclair State and BYU have directors who are chosen through different processes and represent different types of affiliation, and the official governing bodies are composed and selected in different ways, both administrative structures emphasize tripartite representation, along with equity in the decision-making groups. Throughout the history and development of the partnerships and the centers, governance has been flexible and responsive to the developing strengths and needs of the membership.

The University of Texas at El Paso established the El Paso Collaborative for Academic Excellence in 1992. This collaborative did not develop from an existing university-school partnership, although there has always been a form of partnership concerned with the placement of student teachers in the schools. Rather, it was established by the university's administration with a very ambitious agenda of systemic reform across P–16 in the El Paso region. The El Paso Collaborative brought together the superintendents of the three largest districts (representing 130,000 students), the president of the community college, the heads of the chambers of commerce of El Paso and Juarez, the mayor of El Paso, the county judge, and the head of the major grassroots community organization in the region. The board has been meeting bimonthly since 1992, with the university president as the chair. The provost of the university and the dean of the College of Education have regularly attended and actively participated in the El Paso Collaborative board's meetings since its inception. Although the mayor and the judge have stopped attending the meetings, they have sent representatives. An executive director, who reports to the president, manages the collaborative. The simultaneous renewal agenda lies within the collaborative's central mission of improving the academic achievement of all students in the region. A strong tripartite partnership among the College of Education, the colleges of arts and sciences, and the public schools has developed as a major focus within the El Paso Collaborative's systemic reform agenda. Like the officially established centers of pedagogy, this structure includes tripartite representation; enjoys the support of a variety of stakeholders, including the university administration; and shares an agenda focused on the simultaneous renewal of teacher education and public schooling. With many characteristics of a center of pedagogy, the partnership is enjoying many of a center's advantages.

Secure Funding and Resources

All of the settings represented in the case studies in Part Two have worked purposefully to develop new organizational structures that maximize the potential success of the renewal agenda and at the same time establish a base of secure funding to enable them to maintain and continue their activities. All have secured external grants as well as internal institutional funding, sometimes through grant-matching requirements, to build a reliable base of support. Both BYU and Montclair have moved faculty resources and institutional funds into the control of their centers of pedagogy.

In 1998, the Center for the Improvement of Teacher Education and Schooling at BYU was operating with an annual budget of approximately $1 million, and Montclair's Center of Pedagogy had a budget of approximately $800,000. Sorting out contributions from the school districts, the colleges, and the general university budget is complicated, but in every case it is clear that significant funds have been moved toward control by the centers.

The El Paso story is even more complicated. The El Paso Collaborative, although funded with a limited institutional base of $150,000 per year, has been successful in securing multiyear funding from foundations. In 1998, it was operating with a budget of approximately $4 million per year and a staff of twenty-five, all focused on the systemic reform agenda across the region. This funding was independent of substantial contributions by the school districts or separate external grants to the Colleges of Education and Science that were directly associated with the simultaneous renewal agenda. The Colleges of Education and Science, for example, share a five-year, $5 million grant from the National Science Foundation to collaborate with the community college and the public schools in preparing better math and science teachers at the elementary and secondary levels.

A Final Reflection

The experiences of the three collaborative structures illustrate specific organizations generated by and responsive to individual needs and circumstances unique to their settings. Thus, they are different in administrative, operational, and budgetary details. But the three are also products of common challenges and needs. All have been successful in bringing together participants from a college of education, departments of the arts and sciences, and public schools in a wide range of districts to focus on the simultaneous renewal of teacher education and public schooling. Systemic programs have ranged from distance education certification in English as a Second Language to multidistrict critical-thinking instruction; administrative adaptations have ranged from a total revision of a university's definition of scholarship and faculty rewards to the creation of new university faculty positions to be filled by teachers from the schools on a two-year rotation. Funding arrangements are sometimes as creative as the programs and rewards. But with goals and values common to the tripartite membership and with mutual respect, trust, and consideration, these structures are accomplishing effective renewal across a broad range of issues.

Current Conditions, Essential Qualities, and Lessons for the Future

John Goodlad first proposed the idea of a center of pedagogy in his 1990 book, *Teachers for Our Nation's Schools,* and described the creation of a fictional center in a chapter entitled "Renewal at Northern State University: A Fable."[1] However, Goodlad did not intend that centers of pedagogy remain a fable, and they have not. As the concept goes beyond fable status to the establishment of operating centers, several questions become pertinent: To what extent is the idea taking hold? Which promising developments bear watching? How can we gauge the degree of the concept's implementation? This chapter provides some answers to these questions.

Survey of Movement Toward Centers of Pedagogy

In an effort to understand teacher educators' reactions to the concept of a center of pedagogy, the authors conducted a survey of the thirty-four institutions of higher education affiliated with the National Network for Educational Renewal (NNER), and all colleges and universities holding membership in the American Association of Colleges for Teacher Education (AACTE) that reported one hundred or more students in their basic teacher education programs as of 1996. The survey questionnaire, reproduced in the Appendix at the end of this book, was sent to the deans of the institutions.

More than three hundred were mailed; the response rate was 86 percent from the NNER sites and 27 percent from the other institutions.

Deans or their appointed respondents were asked questions that revealed their knowledge of the concept, their plans for implementation, the degree to which critical functions of a center of pedagogy were carried out at their institutions, the roles they considered for the tripartite in teacher education, and the reward systems in place at their institutions and in their partner schools. They were invited to comment about each question and to provide information about practices that they thought either achieved the goals of a center of pedagogy or were moving in that direction. The descriptions of promising practices found later in this chapter are all derived from questionnaire responses or follow-up discussions based on those responses.

Survey Results

Responses to the survey revealed a good deal of familiarity with the concept, with 95 percent of NNER respondents reporting that they were very familiar with the concept, and the remainder indicating that they were somewhat familiar with the idea. At institutions not affiliated with the NNER, 57 percent were very familiar and 29 percent were somewhat familiar. Only 4 percent described themselves as not at all familiar with the concept. Clearly, the concept is widely known at NNER sites and at other institutions nationwide.

Respondents were next asked what actions had been implemented or planned that were affected by their familiarity with the concept. Of the NNER sites reporting, 65 percent noted having in place an administrative structure that was fulfilling the functions of a center of pedagogy, and all but three sites expected to have one by the year 2000. Among sites not affiliated with the NNER, 18 percent reported having such structures; of those not having such structures in place, 23 percent expected to have them by the year 2000. Overall, then, nearly 100 percent of the NNER sites and about 36 percent of other institutions indicated that administrative structures fulfilling the functions of centers of pedagogy were in place or would be in place by the year 2000.

Beyond the existence or anticipation of actual centers or similar structures, the survey asked about the thoughts and experiences of the respondents concerning some of the key ideas associated with such centers. The responses indicate that the idea of simultaneous renewal of teacher education and public schooling has won wide acceptance. At both NNER and non-NNER sites, more than 80 percent reported an institutional commitment to this goal. In nearly as many settings—80 percent of NNER sites and 71 percent of the others—there was a commitment to move toward involving the tripartite—the three faculties in arts and sciences departments, colleges of education, and public schools—in such renewal efforts.

Despite the perception that structures similar to centers of pedagogy are in place, or will be in a few years, the survey revealed a considerable gap between existing conditions at the institutions and what has been revealed through experience and research to be important in their development.

Shared Vision

One quality found to be essential in each of the centers examined in this book is a shared vision among education faculty, arts and sciences faculty, and school faculty regarding the purposes of schools in the United States and ways that educators should be prepared to fulfill these purposes. Only 40 percent of the NNER sites reported that a critical mass of tripartite faculty shared a common vision. The percentage in other institutions was only slightly less—about 37 percent. The survey mailed to the institutions not affiliated with the NNER did not ask that the shared vision be stated, but selected interviews subsequent to the survey revealed a wide variety of visions held by teacher educators, most of them focused on the economic functions of preparation for employment and higher income. NNER sites showed more homogeneous expectations, emphasizing preparation of students for their roles as citizens in a social and political democracy. In other words, NNER deans seemed more likely to define better schools as those leading to better citizenship, while others seemed more likely to define better schools as those leading to better jobs.

A common vision focused on "better schools for better citizens" is far more difficult to articulate and agree on than a focus on "better schools for better jobs." Institutions reporting that the citizenship vision was shared among the tripartite found that a good deal of effort, time, and sustained interaction was required for agreement. Nevertheless, with only 40 percent in either group reporting a critical mass with a shared vision, there is a good distance to go in most settings to achieve this important criterion.

Discussions with respondents, as well as their answers to the questionnaire, showed that they recognized this as a difficult and critical criterion to meet. Some responses suggested doubt that shared vision could be achieved. One dean commented, "I doubt that two people in any of the categories at our institution have a common vision for schooling in the United States." Another dean, new to her position, said, "A common vision. Very hard to achieve. There is a commitment to work together and a common value for school improvement." Not surprisingly, most believed that a common vision was possible among education faculty, less likely among school faculty, and still less likely among faculty in the arts and sciences.

Inquiry

A number of questions probed the kinds of inquiry carried on by the sites indicating that they had structures similar to centers of pedagogy. Inquiry—into the purposes of education and schooling, the effectiveness of the particular preparation program, and teaching and learning—is essential to a center of pedagogy. NNER settings and other settings that reported having structures similar to centers of pedagogy indicated some inquiry into all three domains. Inquiry into the purposes of education and schooling was reported for 65 percent of the NNER sites and 58 percent of the others. At NNER sites, respondents noted inquiry into the effectiveness of their own programs for 85 percent of the sites, with such inquiry being reported for 66 percent of other sites. Among NNER sites, 80 percent pursue inquiry into teaching and learning, and 60 percent of the other sites carry out such inquiry. According to the definition and purpose of a fully functioning center of pedagogy, all three kinds of inquiry must be ongoing through the efforts of education faculty, arts and sciences faculty, and school faculty. Survey responses therefore raise doubts about the legitimacy of some institutions' claims to having a center of pedagogy or similar structure.

Service for Improving Teaching

The survey inquired about service focused on improving teaching among all three members of the tripartite. It was expected that all centers of pedagogy would, in pursuit of simultaneous renewal, be engaged in service of this kind for all members. In the NNER sites reporting, 75 percent said that they provided service focused on the improvement of teaching among school-based faculty, while 55 percent of non-NNER sites reported such service. Among the NNER sites, 70 percent provide service for the improvement of teaching among education faculty, and 51 percent of non-NNER sites do so. Of the NNER sites responding to the survey, 65 percent indicated that they provided for the improvement of teaching among arts and science faculty, and 26 percent of the responding non-NNER sites indicated attempting such improvement.

Rewards

Deans at the various institutions surveyed were asked if faculty engaged in work in the partnership were rewarded for their efforts. Results indicated that education faculty working toward the renewal of P–12 schools were more likely to be rewarded in NNER sites, with 80 percent reporting that they were rewarded for such work, and only 53 percent of the non-NNER sites reporting that education faculty were so rewarded. The disparity is smaller concerning rewards for other members of the tripartite, but the number of sites reporting any rewards was quite low. At NNER sites, only 20 percent of the deans responded that arts and sciences faculty were rewarded for their work in P–12 schools; at non-NNER sites the number was 14 percent. According to the deans surveyed, school faculty engaged in partnership work were also not likely to be rewarded. At NNER sites, 20 percent reported rewards for school faculty, while 30 percent of non-NNER sites reported rewards.

Typical comments in interviews and in open-ended responses regarding rewards for education faculty focused on the absence of support. Specific statements included the following: "Lots of talk, but we don't have nearly enough [support] as we should," and "Only intrinsically." Several lamented a decline in support: "We used to have load time, but with faculty attrition and legislative budget cuts, we no longer have that luxury. Faculty continue their work in schools, but only because they consider it important, not because they are rewarded for it." A number of individuals, however, noted increasing attention to the need for linking criteria for tenure and promotion to work in schools.

For arts and sciences faculty, it was even more common for respondents to identify intrinsic rewards or rewards in the form of pay and released time rather than rewards embedded in criteria for tenure or promotion. Specific examples of criteria for tenure and promotion related to school-based work were absent. One respondent observed, "We do have a number of faculty involved, especially in the sciences, but most of the work is being done by a few faculty." These conditions were implicit in a number of other responses: that it is more common for science faculty to work in schools, they are rewarded intrinsically or directly by compensation, and a few individuals do most of the work. A revealing comment in about 10 percent of the open-ended responses and a common statement in interviews was an admission that the deans of education did not know if arts and sciences faculty were rewarded for school-based partnership work. When asked specifically if arts and sciences faculty were rewarded for their work in P–12 schools, many replied, "I don't even know" or "I haven't a clue." The response reveals a lack of connection between education and arts and sciences faculty.

Regarding public school faculty being rewarded, a surprising number (25 percent) of education faculty who were interviewed reported that they did not know if any reward system existed. Considering these individuals' responses that their institutions had "strong" partnerships, one wonders just how strong the partnerships were. Some deans reported that the primary reward for public school faculty was being associated with the university. Several reported opportunities to participate in seminars or take graduate courses. Certainly these are tangible rewards, but they do not reflect the goals of parity and equity. Of course, part of this disparity grows from the absence of career ladders in most schools. Some university faculty could not even guess what sorts of rewards might be provided for school faculty. One said, "I can't imagine what you mean by rewards for school faculty. Pats on the back? Yes."

Financial Support

Strong partnerships between universities and schools are widely reported, with 80 percent of the NNER sites and 70 percent of the others claiming to have them. Strong support from school and university leadership for partnership work was reported from 90 percent of the NNER sites and 76 percent of the other sites. But probing and follow-up interviews called some of these responses into question. For example, the most common of the open-ended responses, among the 20 percent of the respondents who chose to provide them, suggested that the "support" did not extend to fiscal support. As one respondent noted, "There is strong support and encouragement. This, however, does not translate into the dollars needed." Another said, "Lots of talk, little action, and no money." Still another remarked, "The dean is supportive, as is the new interim vice president for academic affairs. The chancellor seems supportive, but financial support on any level is absent."

Overall Conclusions

The results of this survey indicate widespread knowledge of the center of pedagogy concept, as well as interest in its implementation, with some promising activity under way. However, as with many other significant innovations, there is a danger that the concept will be implemented in form only, without the elements necessary for effective operation. The survey results showed that some institutions reported the presence of structures similar to a center of pedagogy but claimed no significant role in the education of educators for school-based or arts and sciences faculty, little or no inquiry into critical areas, little attention to the enhancement of teaching, and an absence of rewards, especially for arts and sciences and school-based personnel. They reported verbal support but not concrete fiscal support, a situation that does not inspire optimism.

Promising Developments

Despite discouraging results on many aspects of the survey, examination of existing practice has shown that a number of institutions have developed centers of pedagogy or similar structures that are proving effective in coordinating the efforts of college of education faculty, arts and sciences faculty, and public school personnel in the simultaneous renewal of teacher preparation and public school education. Some of the most promising are reviewed in this section.

Winthrop University

At Winthrop University in Rock Hill, South Carolina, an entity called the Center for Pedagogy operates within the College of Education, but with full involvement of professional development school faculty, arts and sciences faculty, and education faculty. The university reports that a critical mass has developed a shared vision, that formal recognition for education faculty working in schools has been provided, and that arts and sciences faculty are rewarded for their work in schools, although not explicitly. The connection with the schools is through a formal partnership, the Winthrop Olde English Consortium, now more than twenty years old.

Furman University

Furman University in Greenville, South Carolina, has a structure called the Forum for Educational Inquiry. Described as a "virtual center of pedagogy," this unit includes faculty in the arts and sciences, education, and the partner schools. The director reports that it is "virtual" because it does not administer teacher education, but it is an integral part of the program.

The Forum is committed to a view of teacher preparation and professional development as functions of the entire university, the public schools, and the community. Supported by the BellSouth Foundation, the Forum is a center for research and inquiry into the art and science of teaching and learning and for the development of effective educational practice. The following goals reported by the Forum suggest that it has the qualities of a center of pedagogy:

- Faculty and students from the arts and sciences, education, and partner schools will engage in research and inquiry projects that will benefit the quality of education provided in the schools and university.

- Faculty representing the tripartite will actively participate in faculty development activities designed to transform teaching in the schools and university to the benefit of all students.

- Forum coordinators will serve as initiators of renewal within the schools and university in an effort to enrich the educational experiences of all students.

- Forum coordinators will actively participate in the improvement of recruitment and selection procedures and the preparation program of preservice

teachers to become reflective leaders in a democratic society for the twenty-first century.

- The organization and governance of the Forum will
  be structured to effectively lead the implementation
  of research and inquiry, faculty development, school
  and university renewal activities, and teacher preparation exemplary of a model support site for other
  liberal arts colleges and their partner schools.[2]

The Forum is composed of a director from the Education Department; three associate directors, representing graduate studies,
arts and sciences, and the schools; and coordinators from arts and
sciences departments, public schools, and the education faculty.

Furman is confronting the issues of governance that every center of pedagogy must face, as well as the issue of the meaning of
membership. Leaders are asking how to keep membership open to
those needed for the process but at the same time to make it meaningful for the ongoing work of the center.

In response to the questionnaire, Furman reported a strong commitment to simultaneous renewal through three-way collaboration,
to a critical mass with a common vision representing all three groups,
and to rewards for faculty geared to their work in the partnership.

California Polytechnic State University

From the beginning of its membership in the NNER, California
Polytechnic State University at San Luis Obispo, California, has
featured an organizational structure akin to a center of pedagogy,
known as the University Center for Teacher Education (UCTE).[3]
The university does not have a college of education; the UCTE
is responsible for teacher education. Voting members include unit
faculty, who are equivalent to education faculty members, with retention, tenure, and promotion processes occurring entirely within
UCTE; single-subject advisers, who coordinate secondary programs
within arts and sciences programs and are jointly members of their
academic departments and the UCTE; and a partner school teacher-

in-residence, who is a full-time voting member for a two-year term. Additional members are content educators: members of academic departments who teach courses to teacher education candidates and are appointed on a yearly basis to the UCTE but without voting rights.

The Coalition of Partner Schools is an organizing structure that is connected to but not a part of the UCTE and coordinates the work of the partner schools in three districts working with the university. Within the Coalition of Partner Schools, an entity called Keepers of the Vision helps to oversee the growth and development of the Coalition and to broaden and deepen the dialogue and the renewal program at each site.

An ongoing issue at Cal Poly has been the status of the director of the UCTE, including her interaction with others described as "deans." To address this, the university has reclassified her position so it is comparable to those heading schools and colleges. The university reports that faculty in all three groups of the tripartite are rewarded for their work in the partnership. There is a high level of university commitment to simultaneous renewal.

University of Hawaii at Manoa
Hawaii School University Partnership

Since 1986, the University of Hawaii at Manoa College of Education (COE) and the Hawaii Department of Education (DOE) have joined forces in the Hawaii School University Partnership. Through this vehicle, the school district and the university have worked on a number of projects related to renewing both teacher preparation and public school education. The following are specific objectives of this partnership:[4]

- Support the faculty and administration of the College of Education and the Department of Education in restructuring the various teacher education programs and facilitating their implementation in partner schools

- Support research and evaluation related to describing the effectiveness of teacher education programs that have been identified as partnership programs
- Support reorganization in the College of Education and the development of the Center for Educational Partnerships [established in 1998 as the Hawaii Institute for Educational Partnerships]

The partnership has sought to build a critical mass through the Hawaii leadership associates program. Partnership officials say, "The underlying philosophy and the moral grounding of the mission of teacher education in a social and political democracy need to be continually affirmed, especially as the circle of involvement widens to include school teachers and principals, district and state education staff, and arts and sciences faculty."[5]

In 1998 the Hawaii School University Partnership was incorporated into a new entity, the Hawaii Institute for Educational Partnerships. State legislation passed in 1994 asked the University of Hawaii at Manoa to establish a "Center for Teacher Education." The initial legislation carried no appropriation, but funding was provided in 1997 as part of a match for a DeWitt Wallace–Reader's Digest Fund Incentive Award in Teacher Education, obtained through the Institute for Educational Inquiry. The original name, Center for Teacher Education, was changed to Institute for Educational Partnerships.

A foundational document prepared for the implementation of the institute indicates its major functions:

> To assist University faculty and DOE teachers and administrators in developing and sustaining school partnerships for the purposes of preparing educators, professional development of in-service teachers, and school renewal. . . .
>
> To ensure that professional education rests on a strong scholarly base, the Institute will also encourage and sup-

port research and inquiry on teaching, learning, professional education, school renewal, and educational reform as these topics are pursued through partnerships. Drawing upon the research and expertise of COE faculty involved in field-based programs, other university faculty, and DOE teachers and staff, the Institute will promote the integration of educational research and practice.[6]

The institute was founded as a semiautonomous unit through a memorandum of agreement between the College of Education and the Department of Education. It is governed by an executive board that includes, at a minimum, the dean of education and the Hawaii superintendent of schools. An institute advisory council includes representatives from the Department of Education, the College of Education, and the colleges of arts and sciences. A director oversees activities and projects conducted by the institute.[7] In many respects the institute assumes the role of a center of pedagogy, the first established by state legislative action.

University of Connecticut

At the University of Connecticut at Storrs, a Center of Pedagogy exists within the School of Education. The Center, with codirectors, is governed by a steering committee from the School of Education, which includes department heads, associate and assistant deans, the dean, and faculty involved in teacher preparation. The steering committee is being expanded to include faculty in the arts and sciences, as well as faculty from the thirty partner schools within the university's nine professional development centers. More than 80 percent of the School of Education faculty are involved in teacher education.[8]

University of Colorado at Denver

The University of Colorado at Denver has developed a comprehensive definition of a center of pedagogy toward which it is working.

Currently three entities fulfill some of the functions of the anticipated center.

First, the Initial Teacher Education Council (ITEC), with thirty-nine members, has approximately equal representation from the university and the schools. University representatives are the professors from the School of Education who work in partner schools and the associate dean for teacher education, who chairs the group. This council functions as the governance body of the Initial Teacher Education Program, making changes in curriculum, decisions about partner school work, and the like. It engages in professional development and conducts business meetings. Work groups have been designated for the following purposes:

- To identify communication modes that will most efficiently and effectively cross school and university

- To ensure that teacher education candidates are better prepared in K–12 schools and in course work to support literacy development

- To develop strategies to help clinical teachers become more effective in mentoring teacher candidates

- To identify effective strategies for promoting and finding time for professional development in partner schools

- To better explain elements of the licensure/teaching portfolio process to teacher candidates

The ITEC holds an average of fifteen meetings a year and conducts a yearly retreat devoted to such topics as implementing research about partner schools.

A second group, the Partner Principals, meets monthly with the dean, the associate dean, and an administrator in residence who chairs the meeting. Although it does not have formal decision-making power, the group does communicate its views and influence the agendas of the ITEC. Sample agenda items from the Partner Principals include refining the role of site coordinators, rethinking benefits for teacher interns, and seeking grants to support renewal.

Recently, the Alliance for the Renewal of Education was formed to include the associate deans from the School of Education and the College of Liberal Arts and Sciences, a faculty member from each school and college, and two site coordinators and two district-level personnel from partner districts. The purpose of the alliance is to foster simultaneous renewal and to provide exemplary education for P–12 students, while preparing future teachers for P–12 public schools. Sample agenda items include encouraging participation of liberal arts faculty in partner schools and/or teacher education, seeking grants to support the work, encouraging districts to use partner schools as resources, generating ideas for teaching exchanges across the tripartite, planning evaluation of partner schools, and examining the ways partner school status enhances learning opportunities for P–12 students. The group meets monthly and represents, in the view of university officials, an important step toward a center of pedagogy.

The University of Colorado at Denver has proposed a working concept and goal for a center of pedagogy.[9] It envisions faculty who

1. Are liberal arts professors, school of education professors, and partner school personnel.
2. Work both in the center and in partner schools.
3. Are provided with administrative support by a person with access to central administrators in the university and school districts.
4. Are committed to teacher education.
5. Work within an award system designed to support and recognize their unique work.

The concept looks to a formally established organizational entity that

1. Is in an intermediate position between university and school district(s).
2. Has negotiated and clear decision-making authority.
3. Has a budget from liberal arts, education, and the school districts.

Finally, it envisions an entity with the responsibility to

1. Prepare educators for the moral, ethical, and enculturating responsibilities of teachers in a democratic society.
2. Highlight the centrality of the teacher education mission in a democratic society.
3. Ensure collaboration and integration of the three essentials of teacher education: general education, the study of educational practices, and the guided practice of teaching.
4. Sustain renewal of the three essentials of teacher education and the program itself.
5. Ensure reflective attention to the art and science of teaching, perhaps via providing support to improve teaching.
6. Engage in research and evaluation about:
   - The needs and characteristics of the context for teacher preparation (liberal arts colleges, schools of education, schools and school districts, and "the public")
   - The knowledge, skills, and values that appear necessary to become an effective teacher and how these should be supported in teacher education
   - The effectiveness of the Center's teacher education program
   - Ways that prospective teachers learn and ways they can best be taught

7. Sustain and promote partner schools.
8. Facilitate the entry and induction of program graduates into the teaching profession.

University of Southern Maine

The University of Southern Maine (USM) has both a very strong school-university partnership—the Southern Maine Partnership—and a broadly representative Teacher Education Council, which may be the basis for a center of pedagogy. A new undergraduate program was designed by a tripartite group, providing the basis for further collaboration and for the evolution of a strong common vision. The university reports a reward system for faculty in education, arts and sciences, and the schools. Rewards for faculty at the university may be given for school-based work, provided publications ensue.

Many institutions report teacher education councils as the basis for centers of pedagogy, but few of those reported are as representative as that at USM. The USM Council includes three faculty from each college or school that sponsors a teacher education program at the university and three members from participating public schools. The Council approves and monitors all initial-level teacher education programs, functions as the vehicle for communication among the areas of the university and the public school communities, serves as a forum for discussion on all issues related to teacher education, creates policies and procedures, reviews curricula and course syllabi to ensure consistency with a conceptual framework, examines evaluation data annually, and reviews the accreditation process. In its present form, it continues to work through recommendations to the dean of education, and it is chaired by the director of teacher education.

A second entity, the Center for Teaching, is a university-wide and university-only structure, supporting pedagogy through collaboration among the colleges of the university.

The third entity, the Southern Maine Partnership, is a well-known and strong alliance created, in the words of its stated mission, to "assist in the development, maintenance, and extension of learner-centered schools through teacher development (preservice and in-service) and school restructuring activities."

As reported by the university, all the functions of a center of pedagogy are in place, but as a divided administrative structure. In a sense, a "virtual" center of pedagogy does appear to exist, which bears watching as a likely alternative model.

Columbia College of South Carolina

At Columbia College, an entity known as the "Alliance of Educators: The Center of Pedagogy at Columbia College" has emerged, joining faculty at the college with faculty in ten professional development schools. Administrators at the college report that governance and responsibility for policy, procedures, evaluation, and planning rest with the Alliance. A group of five professional development school faculty, five arts and sciences faculty, five education faculty, and five student advisory members constitute the Alliance. A separate budget is in place.

Indiana University of Pennsylvania

At Indiana University of Pennsylvania (IUP), a formal constitution established the Academy for Teacher Preparation as a unit for bringing together faculty in education with faculty in the arts and sciences who are involved in the preparation of teachers. The Academy has stated the following purposes:

- The provision of a centrally coordinated organization for the administration and improvement of teacher education at IUP
- The identification, recognition, and support of faculty at IUP who are qualified to engage in the instruction and supervision of teacher education candidates
- The provision of coordinated staff development for Academy members and cooperating teachers and faculty of partnership schools

Membership in the Academy is determined by review of credentials by the deans of the departments in arts and sciences and the education dean, using criteria such as work with school-age clients, appropriate terminal degree, scholarly activities, evidence of quality teaching, promotion of critical thinking and problem solving, and other desired qualifications. The constitution requires membership in the Academy for one to be eligible to teach in the program.

This is an interesting experiment, although some elements of a center of pedagogy are clearly missing. The most significant deficit is the parity and responsibility of school-based faculty in the program, although a mechanism for the advisory role of school-based administrators and teachers, the Field and Partnership Advisory Committee, is in place. Nevertheless, the work at IUP, with a commitment to building a shared vision and establishing a structure outside the College of Education, has much in its favor.

University of New Mexico

Faculty at the University of New Mexico have undertaken an effort designed to implement an amalgam of several of Goodlad's critical postulates, especially Postulate Four: the development of "a clearly identifiable group of academic and clinical faculty members for whom teacher education is the top priority" and which is "responsible and accountable for selecting . . . students and monitoring their progress, planning and maintaining the full scope and sequence of the curriculum, continuously evaluating and improving programs, and facilitating the entry of graduates into teaching careers."[10]

As envisioned, the center is to include faculty, teachers, administrators, other educators and professionals, members of the community, graduate and undergraduate students, and high school and elementary students who would come together to debate, discuss, and dream about what the future might be and to prepare competent, qualified, and caring teachers.

The following excerpt from a University of New Mexico document outlines the plan:

The advantages of establishing a Center for Teacher Education at the University of New Mexico include the following: (1) it fits with who we are at this point in our history; (2) it is a flexible structure that can be improved over time and opens up a variety of possibilities; (3) it strengthens the research component of teacher education; (4) it strengthens the involvement of faculty across the college and the university; and (5) it provides faculty with a more flexible approach to their career paths. The disadvantages of establishing a Center for Teacher Education are that it does not guarantee "faculty involvement" in teacher education; and it requires the support of the college's faculty and administration. Our considered opinion is that the advantages outweigh the disadvantages.

The Center for Teacher Education should have the following components:

1. The Center should manage and house the following licensure programs (including the relevant programs in the Partnership and the branch campuses):
   - Early Childhood Multicultural Education
   - General Elementary Education
   - General Middle School Education
   - General Secondary Education
   - Elementary Education/Special Education Dual Licensure Program
   - Special Education

   "Manage," in this context, means working with faculty, programs (undergraduate and graduate), and divisions in coordinating the doctoral students, resource teachers, and part-time staff that supervise the students; organizing admissions, advising, and student teaching; and facilitating the other administrative and logistical aspects of these programs.

2. The Center should facilitate the following initial licensure teacher education programs:
   - Art Education
   - Health Education
   - Physical Education

   "Facilitate," in this context, means working with the faculty, programs, and divisions associated with these programs to find ways of providing additional support and assistance.

3. The Center should engage in research and evaluation in teacher education. The purpose of the component would be to facilitate research on key topics by UNM faculty and doctoral students, as well as supporting teacher research. The Center would engage in systematic evaluation of our teacher preparation programs; provide critical information to NCATE and other accreditation reviews; provide opportunities to support research; facilitate grant writing and grant acquisition; provide technical help in conducting and publishing research; produce newsletters, occasional papers, and policy briefs. Participation in and support from the research component of the Center is available to all faculty within the college and the university. This would be a great opportunity to strengthen UNM's role at the state level and provide research opportunities for many new faculty and doctoral students.

4. The Center should facilitate a think tank comprised of regular and clinical faculty who work in Art Education; Music Education; Early Childhood Education; Elementary Education; Math, Science, Environmental/Recreational and Technology

Education; Special Education; Bilingual/TESOL
[Teachers of English to Speakers of Other Lan-
guages]/ESL [English as a Second Language] Education; Language Arts Education; Middle School
Education, Secondary Education; Health Education; and Physical Education; *as well as* the other
programs (e.g., Family Studies, Counseling, Educational Leadership) in the college that impact or are
interested in having an impact on teacher education. These faculty would focus on a variety of crucial topics including the development of a clear
and common vision of good teaching that is apparent in all course work and clinical experiences.

5. The Center should facilitate relationships between
faculty in the College of Education and faculty in
other colleges across the university in order to
strengthen and broaden UNM commitment to
teacher education.

6. The Center should facilitate a variety of professional development initiatives and opportunities
for teachers across the state.

7. The Center should facilitate a community and
business involvement with public schools.[11]

University of Missouri, Columbia

The University of Missouri at Columbia's Undergraduate Teacher
Development Center (UTDC) is similar to a center of pedagogy.
Literature prepared by the UTDC reports that, historically, colleges
of education claim to determine what is required in a teacher education program, when in fact such a program is also determined by
public schools and faculty in the arts and sciences. The UTDC is a
collaborative endeavor in which the College of Education joins
with educators from the public schools and the arts and sciences in
redesigning teacher education.

Georgia's Statewide Initiative

Under the auspices of the Georgia Board of Regents, public universities in Georgia have been encouraged through ongoing professional development meetings, grant opportunities, and long-range development plans to undertake *co-reform*, which means a joining together of arts and sciences, education, and school faculty to promote simultaneous renewal. Although no specific administrative structure is required to accomplish this end, universities in Georgia are expected to move toward many of the qualities of centers of pedagogy. In April 1998, the Georgia Board of Regents approved a new set of principles for the preparation of educators and followed this with the approval of a set of actions in July 1998. Two of these principles and related actions virtually mandate center of pedagogy–like structures. Principle 5 states, "Teacher preparation programs will be the shared responsibility of education faculty, arts and sciences faculty, and classroom teachers in the schools." Among the actions recommended under this principle are that each institution establish a functional unit with comparable representation from the tripartite. Principle 6 says, "Through partnership with P–12 schools, universities that prepare teachers will have an ongoing responsibility to collaborate with schools in mentoring, induction, and professional development programs for classroom teachers and school leaders."[12] Thus, shared responsibility for simultaneous renewal—or co-reform, as it is known in Georgia—is mandated by state policy. This is the first statewide initiative outside the NNER to undertake systematic simultaneous renewal of teacher education and the schools with strong participation by arts and sciences faculty.[13]

Indicators of the Essential Qualities

Many complex educational changes have been adopted in name only, or have been implemented so superficially that the essence of the innovation was lost. Think back, for example, to the new mathematics and sciences of the 1960s, individual education models of the 1970s, and implementations of critical-thinking educational models more recently. Clearly, self-reported understanding of the concept of a center of pedagogy is widespread, and many of the institutions reporting implementation of the idea have made significant progress.

This section proposes some standards and indicators to help in the implementation of a center of pedagogy. The indicators are not intended to be a complete list of evidence one might look for in mature centers of pedagogy, nor are they prescriptions for all such centers. They are suggested as representative examples that give evidence that essential qualities are in place. All the indicators can be found within the case studies provided in this book.

QUALITY 1: *There is a common vision within the center, resulting in a set of beliefs and convictions shared by the tripartite—faculty in education, arts and sciences, and schools—regarding the public and private purposes of schools in a democracy. This set of beliefs and convictions guides the design, implementation, and evaluation of educational programs at all levels in the public schools and in the education of educators.*

Indicators

1.1   There is evidence of attention, over time, to the development of a clear shared vision, along with related beliefs and convictions.

1.2   Meetings have occurred among all three members of the tripartite dedicated to the development of shared convictions.

1.3   The common beliefs are evident in statements of the program mission for both school and university partners, including catalogue statements and promotional materials used by the partnership institutions, and are the bases for the mission of the center.

1.4   The common beliefs guide important program decisions, including admission and continuous assessment of students.

1.5   The common vision, or support for the key principles of the vision, is considered in the selection and evaluation of faculty and members of the center.

1.6   Curriculum design includes the common convictions as part of the instructional program of the institutions; these convictions are considered in the evaluation of students at all levels.

1.7   A comprehensive effort to communicate the beliefs of the center to the public is undertaken.

1.8   The degree of consistency between the shared vision and actions of the institutions constituting the center is examined regularly and systematically.

1.9   The center is open to review of the shared vision and the resulting beliefs and convictions; these beliefs and their continued relevance to the center's mission are periodically examined.

1.10 The vision is not imposed, but rather develops using the principles of democracy that call for an openness and sensitivity to alternative perspectives and interpretations, with dialogue maintained until consensus is reached.

1.11 The shared beliefs and commitments are evident in the language and behavior of the members of the center. (Members' words and actions demonstrate the commitment to equity and democracy. For example, university people are not referred to as "faculty" if school-based educators are called "teachers." Such words imply and reinforce status differences.)

QUALITY 2: *Inquiry is central to the work of the center.*

Indicators

2.1   Ongoing inquiry is a commitment of all members of the tripartite.

2.2   Inquiry is undertaken jointly by members of the tripartite.

2.3   Inquiry into the nature and purpose of education in a democracy is evident.

2.4   Inquiry into the most effective pedagogical and curricular approaches for the education of all students is evident.

2.5   Inquiry into the effectiveness of the institutions' programs in educating students according to the shared beliefs and convictions is evident. Such inquiry focuses both on the elements of the program and on the student learning that is accomplished.

2.6   The results of inquiry are used to strengthen educational programs.

2.7   Inquiry and scholarship are defined broadly to include scholarship applied to solving significant problems of educational systems and to improving pedagogy, and such scholarship is valued and rewarded.

QUALITY 3: *The partnership that joins the tripartite of faculty in the P–12 schools, arts and sciences, and education is based on a history of collaboration, mutual trust, shared vision, mutual interests, and parity.*

Indicators

3.1   Partnership among the tripartite has evolved over time, so that parties know and respect each other and each other's work. Opportunities to build this respect are provided regularly.

3.2   The differing needs of the partners are taken into account and are acknowledged so that mutual interests are known.

3.3   Expectations of members of the partnership are known and are, where appropriate, set down in writing.

3.4   The mutual interests of members of the partnership are derived from a common set of beliefs and convictions that are known and explicit.

3.5   Attention to equity is extended to all aspects of the partnership, particularly decision making and the use of language.

3.6   All three groups represented in the partnership contribute resources needed for the center to function.

3.7   The center advocates for equitable reward structures for all three groups represented in the partnership.

3.8   Opportunities for risk taking by individual members of the center are provided so that mutual trust can be developed and sustained.

QUALITY 4: *There is a structure for governance that permits the center to operate in pursuit of its mission.*

Indicators

4.1   Consideration was given to the placement of the center to ensure its independence from all of the tripartite groups and to preserve the independence of the member entities. If placement of the center is within the university structure, care is taken to ensure the protection of the rights and interests of the P–12 participants.

4.2   Structures for reporting relationships are carefully constructed so as not to disfranchise members of the center.

4.3   The structure gives visibility to the center. Its presence is known to members of the educative communities.

4.4   Membership structures are designed to include all whose participation is necessary for accomplishing the mission of the center but maintain appropriate expectations for members.

4.5   Appropriate symbols, such as membership certificates and logos, are used to give identity to the center.

4.6   Membership meetings and events are designed to promote ownership and participation.

4.7   Membership is seen as desirable.

QUALITY 5: *Support from existing leadership of the tripartite members of the center is evident, both through symbols and in resource commitments.*

Indicators

5.1   The beliefs and convictions expressed through the center are shared by leaders of all of the tripartite membership groups.

5.2   Resources to support the center are adequate; resources flow from all membership groups of the center and are provided independently to the center as well.

5.3   Resource contributions by the tripartite include budget as well as time and other resources.

5.4   Leaders of the tripartite report on the importance of the center and include it in their descriptions of important activities.

QUALITY 6: *Positive outcomes attributable to the center are evident and considered important.*

Indicators

6.1   There is a minimum of turf conflict among the tripartite, and that which arises is settled readily because of the common beliefs and convictions.

6.2   Reappointment, tenure, and promotion decisions consider the work that is done through the center.

6.3   Curriculum is not disjointed or plagued by excessive overlap.

6.4   Tension between knowledge and application is minimized, with members of the tripartite understanding the relationship between inquiry and practice.

6.5   Decisions affecting the renewal of teacher education and public schools are clearly the responsibility of the center; center participation is appropriate and expected.

6.6   The performance of future teachers and students related to the mission of the center is measurably improved over time.

In concluding this study of centers of pedagogy, it is appropriate to voice a note of caution because of the rapid growth of the phenomenon. The title *center of pedagogy* may be relatively easy to apply. There is a tendency to attach it quite liberally and almost unconditionally to organizational constructs in order to seem in vogue with currently innovative thought. However, the name without the substance may very well damage or destroy the concept. It is relatively easy to examine other educational reform initiatives and to observe how concepts have been distorted and undermined by abuses in ways they are designated and applied. Thus, as consideration is given to adopting or developing a center of pedagogy, it is important to attend seriously to the essence of the idea rather than to assume that the name may be attached to any practice or structure.

Afterword
The Concept Revisited

John I. Goodlad

The foregoing accounts of three deans regarding progress in their settings toward the creation of centers of pedagogy make a significant caveat abundantly clear: It does not come about overnight. The sources cited for their understanding of the concept specify rather daunting conditions to be put in place, with many of them running counter to conventional practices in teacher education. Not surprisingly, then, much of what they write is about effecting change, and many of the obstacles and sand traps they report are those described in the growing body of literature on serious efforts to effect educational improvement. Consequently, in enhancing our insight into a relatively unexplored and untried concept, they also enrich our awareness of what is likely to be encountered along the way to implementing any idea that threatens prevailing ways.

The conditions to be put in place to implement the concept of centers of pedagogy, as the three authors of this book understand them, are quite unlike the pieces to be put together to create a clearly envisioned and carefully planned product. Even if I had laid out a blueprint for developing the concept, there would necessarily be many variations and deviations among settings endeavoring to follow it, simply because the differences among teacher-preparing institutions and the people conducting them are substantial. This becomes clear in the case study chapters in Part Two; each describes a course characterized by meanders, with some of these meanders serving as reflective preludes to the next progression. There is here a strong cautionary sign for any group anticipating a fast-track route to achieving a "trophy" center of pedagogy.[1]

It's Old Hat, We've Done That, or It's Untried

It is commonplace to refer to people—usually people older than we are—as being set in their ways. But we have plenty of evidence from many domains of inquiry to show that this hardening is often the accompaniment of new learnings. Yesterday, we struggled to understand Howard Gardner's theory of multiple intelligences. Today, we have reified six or seven of these and quickly pass over Gardner's observation that "these intelligences are fictions—at most, useful fictions—for discussing processes and abilities that are . . . continuous with one another."[2] John Dewey feared that twenty years of teaching experience too often represents the first year repeated twenty times.

There is no greater obstacle to welcoming the new than addiction to the old. This is not something, however, that should too readily arouse wrath and condemnation. The significant learnings that dominate in our daily behaviors—especially those most noted in the public domain—did not come easily. When they become institutionalized in our work, the price of challenging and moving away from them comes high. Since being set in one's ways is an attribution we prefer to avoid, we seek to clothe the threatening call to change in unflattering garb. Some of us become expert in this art of deflection.

In my many years of flirting with and observing the fate of proposals for change in education—some of them appearing to be eminently sensible and well founded—one or more of three types of deflection appear to me to have dominated over all others: the "it's old hat" syndrome, the "we've done that" or "we are doing it" syndrome, and the "it's untried" syndrome. Of the three, I find the "we've done that" syndrome to be the most insidious because it is so often deceptive of both self and others.

In anticipation of attending a national conference during the year following publication of our book, *The Nongraded Elementary School* (1959), Robert Anderson and I announced a meeting of representatives of schools reporting to be engaged in nongrading. Close to one hundred of these showed up, some simply out of interest in the concept but more than fifty to testify to ongoing work. We secured the names and addresses of those so testifying and followed up with a detailed questionnaire. Out of the embarrassment of having nothing of substance to report, most did not respond. From the data supplied by the others, it was clear that fewer than a half-dozen were seriously engaged in anything justifying the nongraded label. Later, a doctoral dissertation reporting visits to schools claiming nongradedness concluded that there was only one in the United States warranting that claim but another well on the way. The hype and faddishness of school reform invite both witting and unwitting deception.

In commenting on my fictitious account of the creation of a center of pedagogy in the concluding chapter of *Teachers for Our Nation's Schools*, my colleague Kenneth Sirotnik advised me not to hold my breath while waiting for implementation. He viewed the concept as providing a useful call for closer collaboration among the diverse faculty groups conducting parts of teacher education programs, but had little expectation for the emergence of organizational units along the lines I had described. The appearance of this book nine years later confirms the prescience of his advice as well as an overly pessimistic prediction. And the results of the survey reported in Chapter Eight rule out any credibility for the off-putting claim that the concept is a relic from the past and is now old hat. Clearly, the message Sirotnik viewed as important to convey is not yet frequently viewed as warranting priority attention.

The survey was sent only to institutions affiliated with the National Network for Educational Renewal (NNER) and some member colleges and universities of the American Association of Colleges for Teacher Education (AACTE). There has not been since 1991 an annual conference of the AACTE that did not include reference to the concept of centers of pedagogy in an address, symposium, or special-interest session. Yet only 27 percent of the sites (outside of those in the NNER) responded. It is somewhat encouraging, however, to note that only 4 percent of the sites responding reported no familiarity with the concept.

Given these data, it becomes reasonable to take with a grain of salt the dismissing of centers of pedagogy on the grounds that "we've done that." Even the two deans reporting centers of pedagogy in place (one under a different name) view them as works in progress. So far as I know, theirs are the only existing such organizational structures in place. The fact that several of the sites in the NNER regard the development of a center of pedagogy as a work in progress should come as no surprise. A condition of membership in the NNER is that of working toward close collaboration of the three faculty groups engaged (commonly separately and with little communication) with some major component of teacher education programs: of the arts and sciences, of the school of education, and of the partner schools. In time, as the three case studies in this book make clear, effecting this collaboration increasingly calls for some kind of umbrella under which these groups come together in a common mission. It is gratifying to note the emergence of this response to the message in sites outside of the NNER.

Given the rather obvious lack of credibility in two of the three most common ways of deflecting proposals for changing established ways, we are left only with "it's untried." It is common practice for school districts to send platoons of teachers and administrators, prior to carefully studying a proposed innovation, to visit sites claiming early use. Without clear understanding of and criteria regarding what to look for, they latch onto what is claimed to be implementation of what they are looking for but which may be far removed from the fundamental ideas. Then, later, after trying and then abandoning what they thought they saw, their response to the next encounter with these ideas is, "We've already tried that."

Neither age nor novelty should be the criterion in judging proposals for change. The relevant criteria pertain to both the validity of the key ideas and their relevance to critical problems and issues perceived to require resolution; this validity, in turn, usually depends on the depth and quality of the inquiry from which these ideas emerged. The implications of this last statement should lead interested groups to critical inquiry of their own, particularly disciplined conversation on the part of those on whom implementation ultimately will depend. This is precisely the conversation, taking place in various forms, in which the three settings described in detail in this book have been engaged and continue to be engaged as they seek to understand and implement the concept of centers of pedagogy. In the process, all have learned from voyagers engaged in similar journeys.

As I have stated, a center of pedagogy is not likely to come into existence quickly and full blown. Rather, it is likely to take shape in an ongoing process of seeking coherent teacher education programs. The case studies in this book reveal a progression from the rather obvious importance of school-university linkage in preparing teachers to the less obvious need for the university side to include professors from the arts and sciences as well as from schools of education. The survey reported in Chapter Eight revealed much greater comfort on the part of deans of education with the school of education–school partnership than with the tripartite collaboration I recommend. The self-assessments that are ongoing in NNER settings reveal clearly that there is a long way to go in effecting the arts and sciences–school of education relationship. It may well be that insistence on the involvement of all three groups, each with equal status, constitutes for some teacher-preparing settings the major deterrent in proceeding toward centers of pedagogy. Some of the turf battles regarding authority over various parts of programs have not been pretty and are not easily forgotten. And although the concept of centers of pedagogy addresses some of the persistent, bedrock issues of teacher education, it takes only a modest amount of reflection to envision the route to require much more than casual commitment, an observation confirmed by this book.

Genesis of the Concept

In most arenas of human endeavor, it is dangerous to cite confidently the origins of things, especially ideas. Chapter Nine of my book, *Teachers for Our Nation's Schools* (1990), credits B. Othanel Smith with stimulating my use of "centers of pedagogy" to encompass the concept I outlined. Four years later, in *Educational Renewal: Better Teachers, Better Schools,* I go back to John Dewey's century-old proposal for a department of pedagogy at the University of Chicago. But I am not prepared to say that their proposals constitute the only earlier introductions of or variations on the theme. Certainly, the word *pedagogy* has a long history, and it is possible that some of this history includes elements of what Dewey, Smith, and I had in mind.

What we had in mind, however, is neither a common conception nor a similarly arranged organizational entity. Indeed, Chapter Three of this book states the following: "While it may have its roots in some of the ideas Dewey and Smith put forth, the center of pedagogy proposed by Goodlad is a very different concept." I am pleased to agree because I believe the differences to be sufficiently great as to lead to quite different outcomes. My reading of Dewey[3] and Smith[4] is that both were attuned much more closely and exclusively than I am to the definition of pedagogy and the clear identity of pedagogy as a mansion in the house of academia.

The department of pedagogy Dewey proposed to the trustees of the University of Chicago in 1896 would have extended his laboratory school from its then-primary years to college, thus connecting with and becoming a laboratory in the subsequent "scientific training" of teachers. He was advocating identity and status for the art and science of teaching, arguing that "the first university to undertake this work will, in my judgment, secure the recognition, and, indeed, the leadership of the educational forces of the country."[5] Over a hundred years later, we are still waiting.

Nowhere in my reading of Smith's report do I find such expectations. He appeared to be seeking not a structure that would align the arts and sciences contribution to that of the other two groups participating in teacher education but a sharper, clearer mission for schools of education. His school of pedagogy would have at its core attention to the art and science of teaching. Like Dewey, he perceived the necessity of this attention linking college and university faculty in the school of pedagogy to schools serving as laboratories for practice and inquiry.

Where my proposal for centers of pedagogy clearly overlaps with the proposals of Dewey and Smith is in our common emphasis on pedagogy: the art and science of teaching. For reasons with which I think they would have agreed, I argue against the designation "centers of *teacher education*," which does not connote the inquiry one associates with "centers of *pedagogy*." It is what I add to the concept of the center that probably caused the authors of this book to view my proposal to be "a very different concept." Now I align somewhat with Abraham Flexner's argument in his 1910 report on medical education: the general education curriculum must ensure that the physician will be a well-educated citizen.[6] Depth of understanding and competence in the art and science of teaching is not sufficient for our schoolteachers, who should be among the best-educated citizens in the community. Consequently, it is necessary that the department, school, or center of pedagogy charged with educating teachers have within it the organizational and administrative mechanisms for ensuring programmatic attention to their general education. Thus, in *Educational Renewal: Better Teachers, Better Schools,* I state the following: "It is a setting that brings together and blends harmoniously and coherently the three essential ingredients of a teacher's education: general, liberal education; the study of educational practices; and the guided exercise of the art, science, and skill of teaching."[7]

But there is still another argument for effecting this proposed blending and for addressing the structure necessary to establish the organizational boundaries for its identity and protection. Teaching in schools is a special case of teaching, and it is the only profession that uses the domains of knowledge and both modern and postmodern conceptions of knowledge as its occupational tools. In *Teachers for Our Nation's Schools,* I describe this uniqueness as follows: "Teachers are the only specialists in our society called upon to inculcate, not merely apply, the rules of their expertise. For teachers—whether at elementary, secondary, or tertiary levels—a very large part of these rules constitutes the substance and structure of human experience incorporated over time into the arts and sciences disciplines."[8] Consequently, their experiences with the arts and sciences contribute significantly not only to their own education but also to the professional qualities they bring to the challenge of enculturating the young into our democratic society and the world in which we live.

A center of pedagogy—that is, a place for advancing the art and science of pedagogy—need not be a place solely for educating P–12 teachers. Such a place would be relevant to teaching of all kinds. In meeting with presidents and provosts of the NNER, I have found that they want to know whether such a center would play a part in the improvement of campus teaching generally and might be, for example, a resource for pedagogical assistance to teaching assistants and, indeed, professors. The answer is, of course, yes.

Although I back off from the term *centers of teacher education,* largely because the mixed group of specialists involved tend to focus their inquiry on their own fields, I have no problems with *centers of pedagogy and teacher education.* Indeed, this lengthier wording comes closer than the shorter *centers of pedagogy* to embracing the entire range of inquiry into schooling, teaching, and teacher education characteristic of robust, coherent teacher education programs. It is important to remember that my initial (and continuing) advocacy of centers of pedagogy had its origins in two comprehensive studies: one concluding that teachers in our schools were being short-changed through societal neglect and indifference regarding the chasm between the demands of their jobs and their preparation for them,[9] and the other revealing the degree to which this neglect and indifference, together with other factors, contribute to the inadequate depth, breadth, and coherence of teachers' general and professional education and pedagogical expertise.[10] More and better attention to pedagogy is necessary to but not sufficient for the competency and caring required of teachers seeking, as they must, to balance the development of individuality, responsibility, and respect for appropriate authority in the young. Such a concern overshadows that of devoting more attention to pedagogy alone without obscuring the importance of and need for such a focus.

Concluding Observations on the Journey

Although the three settings featured in Part Two are quite different, the commonplaces encountered are many. By "commonplaces" I mean way points to which all three commonly came on the journey. The similarities in the way points facilitated a summary of common encounters and a substantial list of components of a functioning center of pedagogy. It is interesting to note the extent to which the commonplaces encountered and the components recommended connect back to the concept of centers of pedagogy addressed from several perspectives in the three chapters of Part One.

Although three case studies revealing not only rather clear connections between a general conception and common encounters in endeavoring to implement this conception do not refute Alan Tom's contention, quoted in Chapter One, that "the internal workings of the center are hazy," they do raise an interesting and relatively unstudied question about the change process: What level of specificity in regard to a proposal or design for change most helps interested voyagers? I raised this question about agendas for educational change in the Introduction to *Leadership for Educational*

Renewal: Developing a Cadre of Leaders, Volume One of the series of books in which this one is included.[11]

I disagree with Tom regarding his implication that the "largely untried" state of the concept at the time of his writing was because the details about how "to create, organize and sustain a center for pedagogy" remain vague.[12] There is considerable evidence in sagas of experiences with educational change to suggest that university professors, especially in major research universities, are quick to re-ject anything resembling a blueprint because such threatens their independence of mind and action.

There are other, perhaps more powerful human factors that mo-tivate hesitancy in the face of countervailing proposals for change (even if lacking in details) and in the social and political context in which educators pursue their careers, particularly in higher edu-cation. The case studies document some of these. For example, early in the 1990s, when the three settings were very much involved with the *nonnegotiable* agenda of the NNER, the atmosphere of support for a faculty reward structure relevant to the work was one of untested rhetoric. We were getting evidence to show that many pro-fessors perceived our agenda to threaten rather than enable their research careers and the accompanying rewards. And the pressure of policymakers on university administrators to connect their insti-tutions to the community and especially to the schools was only be-ginning. It is fair to say that without the leadership of the three deans (and, in one case, his predecessors), the journeys toward school-university partnerships, partner schools, and centers of ped-agogy would not have started, and the case studies would never have been written.

Although the major obstacles to productive change are deeply embedded in the psyches of humans and in the traditions, connec-tions, and regularities of institutions, the issue Tom raises regarding the specificity of the concept or agenda presented must not be passed over lightly. Stated vaguely and lacking examples or illus-trations, a concept both deceives the unwary and leaves the fast-adopters to pursue whatever course they wish. Spelling out "the internal workings," on the other hand, ignores individual differences and cramps creativity. Indeed, doing so limits the richness of the variations that emerge.

In introducing centers of pedagogy in the final chapters of *Teachers for Our Nation's Schools*, I rather gently pushed several key actors onto the educational stage to enact what I billed as a fable. (In retrospect, were I to rewrite that chapter, I think I would drop the label. It provided too great an opportunity to shrug off the concept as imaginary or unreal.) Then, fearing that I would be shaking too many cages in developing one of the two organizational models proposed—a structure that created a self-standing entity reporting directly to the provost or academic vice president—I put some clothes on the other: a unit within the existing college of education. Nonetheless, the threat was palpable. At the end of my presentation on our study of teacher education to deans of land grant university schools of education (at the 1991 AACTE Annual Meeting), an insightful dean asked what the rest of the school of education would be doing were the center of pedagogy a part of it. I responded to the effect that I thought, given a little time, I could figure that out, but schools of education needed to do that for themselves or they would be heading for deep trouble.

In *Educational Renewal: Better Teachers, Better Schools*, I fleshed out the concept of the center of pedagogy considerably and, I think, sufficiently, given the degree to which the three settings described in preceding chapters were able to derive a sense of the necessary conditions to be put in place and to proceed toward them in their own ways. And, this time, with the fable having had a run of several years, I gave somewhat more attention than before to the alternative of a self-standing unit embracing a chunk of the college of education, relevant components of the arts and sciences, and partner schools. Unlike some critics of the concept, I regard this alternative to be potentially less threatening to colleges of education than is the other; while facilitating the necessary tripartite collaboration, it removes the appearance (and the reality) of the college of education's calling the shots. I say "less threatening" because the existence of a center of pedagogy inside a college of education does draw attention to the fact that it is but a part of that college, thus inducing the question raised by the dean referred to above: And what will the rest of the college of education be doing?

From the perspective of many people with the power to determine the very existence of colleges of education, teacher education is their only reason for existence—and not a very powerful one at that. This perception often includes the view that the research claimed is puffery and not worth doing. With teacher education in a safer haven than it enjoys today—that is, with the college of education joined in an entity with partners often viewed as better alternatives for the production of teachers, namely, the colleges of arts and sciences and the P–12 schools—colleges of education might then become more aggressive in and focused on justifying their role in research and inquiry. We now have a sufficient fund of knowledge relevant to educational practice to replace the present haphazard, politically driven school reform boondoggles with a steady, cumulative, knowledge-based approach to improvement. Indeed, were the media to devote to education and schooling the resources and investigative talent they commit to what is trivial and titillating in our society, much of the expenditure of public funds on the misguided whims and fancies of individuals in positions of power would be revealed as a national scandal.[13]

I have argued for the redesign of teacher education, with the creation of centers of pedagogy as a major part of that design, almost entirely on moral grounds: the need for comprehensive, coherent preparation programs that ensure for each child and youth well-educated, professionally competent, caring teachers. But moral arguments quite commonly are not adequately persuasive, even in the domain of education, which, rhetorically at least, lays claim to a considerable amount of moral ground.[14]

And so I add a practical argument directed especially toward readers who argue the case for teacher education from a different moral perspective: History shows that most of the caring stewards of teacher education have come not from the schools and not from the arts and sciences but from the departments, schools, and colleges of education. But their continuation in this role is severely threatened, with this threat stemming from the old and, increasingly, some new sources. The popular alternatives are the mentoring of future teachers by present teachers or replacing all of what professors of education do with more of what professors in the arts and sciences do. Obviously, both groups are essential to the education of the teachers we need. Let us bring all three groups together in one tent, be that a center of pedagogy or a center of pedagogy *and* teacher education.

Appendix:
Survey of Institutions
of Higher Education

Name of Setting: _____

Please use the following scale in responding to question 1 and questions 5 through 12 by circling the appropriate number. Feel free to comment after each, *if you wish*.

1	2	3	4	5
Not at All		Somewhat		Very Much So

1. Are you familiar with the concept of
   a Center of Pedagogy as described
   by Goodlad?   1   2   3   4   5

   Comment:

2. Do you now have an entity in place
   that fulfills the functions of a Center
   of Pedagogy?

   Yes _____   No _____

3. If yes, what is it called?

4. If no, do you expect to have such an
   entity by the end of 1999?

   Yes _____   No _____

   Comment:

5. Is your institution committed to the
   concept of simultaneous renewal of
   the schools and the education of
   educators?   1   2   3   4   5

   Comment:

6. Is your institution committed to
   three-way collaboration between the
   faculties in education, the arts and
   sciences, and the P–12 schools to
   accomplish simultaneous renewal?   1   2   3   4   5

   Comment:

7. At your institution, does a critical
   mass of faculty in education, faculty
   in the arts and sciences, and faculty
   in the schools share a common vision
   for the education of educators and
   schooling in the United States?   1   2   3   4   5

   Comment:

8. At your institution, which of the
   following are carried out by an entity
   defined as a Center of Pedagogy?

   a. The initial preparation and
      continued professional
      development of P–12 educators   1   2   3   4   5
   b. Inquiry into the purposes of
      education and schooling   1   2   3   4   5
   c. Inquiry into the preparation
      programs   1   2   3   4   5
   d. Inquiry into your setting's
      particular preparation program   1   2   3   4   5
   e. Inquiry into teaching   1   2   3   4   5
   f. Providing service for the
      improvement of teaching for
      faculty in partner schools   1   2   3   4   5
   g. Providing service for the
      improvement of teaching for
      faculty in the school, department,
      or college of education   1   2   3   4   5
   h. Providing service for the
      improvement of teaching for
      faculty in schools, departments,
      or colleges across campus   1   2   3   4   5

   Comment:

9. At your institution, are education
   faculty rewarded for their work in
   schools?   1   2   3   4   5

   Comment:

10. At your institution, are arts and
sciences faculty rewarded for their
work in schools?   1   2   3   4   5

Comment:

11. Is there a history of strong
partnerships between the university
and the schools?   1   2   3   4   5

Comment:

12. Is there strong support from
leadership of the university and
the schools for work together in
the renewal of schools and the
renewal of teacher education?   1   2   3   4   5

Comment:

13. If you have an entity fulfilling
the functions of a Center of
Pedagogy, please describe it.
We are interested in knowing if
it is separate from the school/
college of education, and anything
else that might be helpful in
understanding your structure
and its governance. Please
attach any descriptions you have.

Is there anything more that you
wish to tell us?

How might we contact you if we
wish to follow up or have questions?

Notes

Series Foreword

1. Theodore Roosevelt, "The Manly Virtues and Practical Politics," *Forum* 17 (July 1894): 551.

2. I explored this relationship in *Morality, Efficiency, and Reform: An Interpretation of the History of American Education*, Work in Progress Series no. 5 (Seattle: Institute for Educational Inquiry, 1995).

3. Neil Postman, *The End of Education: Redefining the Value of School* (New York: Vintage, 1996 [orig. Knopf, 1995]), pp. 5–6.

4. John I. Goodlad, *Educational Renewal: Better Teachers, Better Schools* (San Francisco: Jossey-Bass, 1994), pp. 4–6.

5. John I. Goodlad, *A Place Called School: Prospects for the Future* (New York: McGraw-Hill, 1984); John I. Goodlad, Roger Soder, and Kenneth A. Sirotnik (eds.), *The Moral Dimensions of Teaching* (San Francisco: Jossey-Bass, 1990); John I. Goodlad, Roger Soder, and Kenneth A. Sirotnik (eds.), *Places Where Teachers Are Taught* (San Francisco: Jossey-Bass, 1990); John I. Goodlad, *Teachers for Our Nation's Schools* (San Francisco: Jossey-Bass, 1990); and John I. Goodlad and Pamela Keating (eds.), *Access to Knowledge: An Agenda for Our Nation's Schools* (New York: College Entrance Examination Board, 1990).

By 1997, four more books contributed to the growing literature associated with the Agenda: Goodlad, *Educational Renewal*; Roger Soder (ed.), *Democracy, Education, and the Schools* (San Francisco:

Jossey-Bass, 1996); John I. Goodlad and Timothy J. McMannon (eds.), *The Public Purpose of Education and Schooling* (San Francisco: Jossey-Bass, 1997); and John I. Goodlad, *In Praise of Education* (New York: Teachers College Press, 1997).

6. The postulates were first defined in Goodlad, *Teachers for Our Nation's Schools*, pp. 54–64, and later refined in Goodlad, *Educational Renewal*, pp. 70–94.

Chapter One

1. John I. Goodlad, *Teachers for Our Nation's Schools* (San Francisco: Jossey-Bass, 1990), pp. 307–377.

2. B. Othanel Smith, *A Design for a School of Pedagogy* (Washington, D.C.: U.S. Government Printing Office, 1980).

3. Goodlad, *Teachers for Our Nation's Schools*, p. 350.

4. Goodlad, *Teachers for Our Nation's Schools*, p. 352.

5. Goodlad, *Teachers for Our Nation's Schools*, p. 340.

6. Goodlad, *Teachers for Our Nation's Schools*, p. 373.

7. Christopher J. Lucas, *Teacher Education in America: Reform Agendas for the Twenty-first Century* (New York: St. Martin's Press, 1997), p. 252.

8. Lucas, *Teacher Education in America*, p. 252.

9. Robert N. Bush, "Teacher Education Reform: Lessons from the Past Half Century," *Journal of Teacher Education* 38 (May–June 1987): 15.

10. Seymour B. Sarason, *The Case for Change: Rethinking the Preparation of Educators* (San Francisco: Jossey-Bass, 1993), p. 142.

11. Arthur E. Bestor, *Educational Wastelands: The Retreat from Learning in Our Public Schools* (Urbana: University of Illinois Press, 1953), and *The Restoration of Learning: A Program for Redeeming the Unfulfilled Promise of American Education* (New York: Knopf, 1955).

12. Bestor, *Restoration of Learning*, p. 4.

13. Bestor, *Restoration of Learning*, p. 79.

14. Bestor, *Restoration of Learning*, p. 156.

15. Bestor, *Restoration of Learning*, p. 253.

16. Wayne J. Urban, "Historical Studies of Teacher Education," in W. Robert Houston (ed.), *Handbook of Research on Teacher Education* (New York: Macmillan, 1990), p. 68.

17. Mary Anne Raywid, *The Ax-Grinders: Critics of Our Public Schools* (New York: Macmillan, 1962), p. 1.

18. Raywid, *Ax-Grinders*, p. 2.

19. John I. Goodlad, *Educational Renewal: Better Teachers, Better Schools* (San Francisco: Jossey-Bass, 1994), p. 1.

20. Linda Darling-Hammond and Barnett Berry, *The Evolution of Teacher Policy* (Santa Monica, Calif.: RAND, 1988), p. 5.

21. Carnegie Forum on Education and the Economy, Task Force on Teaching as a Profession, *A Nation Prepared: Teachers for the 21st Century* (New York: Carnegie, 1986), p. 2.

22. National Commission on Teaching & America's Future, *What Matters Most: Teaching for America's Future* (New York: National Commission on Teaching & America's Future, 1996), p. 3.

23. Mary Hatwood Futrell, "The Courage to Change," in Leonard Kaplan and Roy A. Edelfelt (eds.), *Teachers for the New Millennium: Aligning Teacher Development, National Goals, and High Standards for All Students* (Thousand Oaks, Calif.: Corwin, 1996), p. 2.

24. Michael Fullan and others, *The Rise and Stall of Teacher Education Reform* (Washington, D.C.: American Association of Colleges for Teacher Education, 1998), pp. xv–xvi.

25. Alan R. Tom, *Redesigning Teacher Education* (Albany: State University of New York Press, 1997), p. 2.

26. Lucas, *Teacher Education in America*, p. 90.

27. Daniel P. Liston and Kenneth M. Zeichner, *Teacher Education and the Social Conditions of Schooling* (New York: Routledge, 1991), p. 2.

28. National Commission on Teaching & America's Future, *What Matters Most*, p. 24.

29. National Commission on Teaching & America's Future, *What Matters Most*, p. 64.

30. National Commission on Teaching & America's Future, *What Matters Most*, p. vii.

31. Tom, *Redesigning Teacher Education*, p. 8.

32. G. K. Hodenfield and T. M. Stinnett, *The Education of Teachers: Conflict and Consensus* (Englewood Cliffs, N.J.: Prentice-Hall, 1961), pp. ix–x.

33. Hodenfield and Stinnett, *Education of Teachers*, pp. 3–4.

34. Harold O. Rugg, *The Teacher of Teachers: Frontiers of Theory and Practice in Teacher Education* (New York: Harper & Brothers, 1952), p. 19.

35. Hodenfield and Stinnett, *Education of Teachers*, p. 17.

36. Hodenfield and Stinnett, *Education of Teachers*, p. 26.

37. Hodenfield and Stinnett, *Education of Teachers*, p. 26.

38. Melvin W. Barnes, "Building School-University Relations in Teacher Education," in Stanley Elam (ed.), *Improving Teacher Education in the United States* (Bloomington, Ind.: Phi Delta Kappa, 1967), p. 137.

39. Barnes, "Building School-University Relations," pp. 138–139.

40. Barnes, "Building School-University Relations," p. 141.

41. Barnes, "Building School-University Relations," p. 155.

42. James B. Conant, *The Education of American Teachers* (New York: McGraw-Hill, 1963).

43. Tom, *Redesigning Teacher Education*, p. 62.

44. Fullan and others, *Rise and Stall*, p. vii.

45. Thomas J. Lasley, *Issues in Teacher Education*, vol. 2, *Background Papers from the National Commission for Excellence in Teacher Education* (Washington, D.C.: American Association of Colleges for Teacher Education, 1986), p. 212.

46. Futrell, "Courage to Change," p. 7.

47. Gene I. Maeroff, "The Future of Partnerships," *On Common Ground* (Yale–New Haven Teachers Institute) 8 (Winter 1998): 9.

48. Maeroff, "Future of Partnerships," p. 9.

49. Maeroff, "Future of Partnerships," p. 10.

50. Futrell, "Courage to Change," p. 3.

51. Gerald N. Tirozzi, "Partnerships for Today and Tomorrow," *On Common Ground* (Yale–New Haven Teachers Institute) 8 (Winter 1998): 7.

52. Robert V. Bullough and others, "What Matters Most: Teaching for America's Future? A Faculty Response to the Report of the National Commission on Teaching & America's Future," *Journal of Education for Teaching* 24 (April 1998): 23.

53. Zhixin Su, "School-University Partnerships: Ideas and Experiments (1986–1990)," Occasional Paper no. 12 (Seattle: Center for Educational Renewal, University of Washington, 1990), pp. 2–3.

54. Su, "School-University Partnerships," p. 3.

55. Lee Teitel, "Can School-University Partnerships Lead to the Simultaneous Renewal of Schools and Teacher Education?" *Journal of Teacher Education* 45 (September–October 1994): 245–252.

56. Walter Doyle, "Themes in Teacher Education Research," in W. Robert Houston (ed.), *Handbook of Research on Teacher Education* (New York: Macmillan, 1990), p. 7.

57. Lucas, *Teacher Education in America*, p. 162.

58. Mary E. Diez, "Who Will Prepare the Next Generation of Teachers?" in Kaplan and Edelfelt (eds.), *Teachers for the New Millennium*, p. 34.

59. Holmes Group, *Tomorrow's Schools: Principles for the Design of Professional Development Schools* (East Lansing, Mich.: Holmes Group, 1990), pp. 2–3.

60. Holmes Group, *Tomorrow's Schools*, p. 5.

61. Holmes Group, *Tomorrow's Schools*, p. 6.

62. "New Schools of Thought," *New Education* (Michigan State University College of Education) 3 (Fall 1997). Available at http://ed-web3.educ.msu.edu/NewEd/Fall97/new.htm. Accessed October 1998.

63. Andy Hargreaves, "Toward a Social Geography of Teacher Education," in Nobuo K. Shimahara and Ivan Z. Holowinsky (eds.), *Teacher Education in Industrialized Nations: Issues in Changing Social Contexts* (New York: Garland, 1995), pp. 29–30.

64. Fullan and others, *Rise and Stall*, p. 51.

65. Fullan and others, *Rise and Stall*, p. viii.

66. Nancy Zimpher, "A Case for PDSs: A Speech by Dr. Nancy Zimpher," *New Education* (Michigan State University College of Education) 3 (Fall 1997). Available at http://ed-web3.educ.msu.edu/NewEd/Fall97/speech.htm. Accessed October 1998.

67. Goodlad, *Teachers for Our Nation's Schools*, Chap. 8.

68. Tom, *Redesigning Teacher Education*, pp. 219–220.

69. John I. Goodlad, "Sustaining and Extending Educational Renewal," *Phi Delta Kappan* 78 (November 1996): 232.

Chapter Two

1. Theodore L. Gross, *Partners in Education: How Colleges Can Work with Schools to Improve Teaching and Learning* (San Francisco: Jossey-Bass, 1988), p. 24.

2. W. R. Houston, cited by Thomas M. McGowan and James Powell, "Understanding School-University Collaboration Through New Educational Metaphors," *Contemporary Education* 61 (Spring 1990): 113.

3. Cable Starlings and Claudia S. Dybdahl, "Defining Common Ground: A Grass Roots Model for University–Public School Collaboration," *Teacher Education and Special Education* 17 (Spring 1994): 106.

4. Mary Christenson and others, "Collaboration in Support of Change," *Theory into Practice* 35 (Summer 1996): 187.

5. McGowan and Powell, "Understanding School-University Collaboration," p. 113.

6. Sarah Dawn Smith, "Professional Partnerships and Educational Change: Effective Collaboration over Time," *Journal of Teacher Education* 43 (September–October 1992): 243.

7. Nancy Winitzky, Trish Stoddart, and Patti O'Keefe, "Great Expectations: Emergent Professional Development Schools," *Journal of Teacher Education* 43 (January–February 1992): 9.

8. C. Garn Coombs and J. Merrell Hansen, "Lessons Learned," *Educational Horizons* 68 (Summer 1990): 216.

9. Winitzky, Stoddart, and O'Keefe, "Great Expectations."

10. Susan M. Brookhart and William E. Loadman, "School-University Collaboration: Across Cultures," http://www.teachingeducation.com/42fa.htm, p. 2. Accessed July 1998.

11. Judith Haymore Sandholtz and Ellen C. Finan, "Blurring the Boundaries to Promote School-University Partnerships," *Journal of Teacher Education* 49 (January–February 1998): 18.

12. Sandholtz and Finan, "Blurring the Boundaries," p. 18.

13. Thomas J. Lasley, Thomas J. Matczynski, and James A. Williams, "Collaborative and Noncollaborative Partnership Structures in Teacher Education," *Journal of Teacher Education* 43 (September–October 1992): 258.

14. Maria E. Torres-Guzman, with Lourdes I. Ivory and others, "Stories About Differences in a Collaboration with Middle School Students," *Theory into Practice* 35 (Summer 1996): 204.

15. Sidney Trubowitz, "What Works and What Gets in the Way," *Educational Horizons* 68 (Summer 1990): 214.

16. Coombs and Hansen, "Lessons Learned," p. 216.

17. McGowan and Powell, "Understanding School-University Collaboration," p. 114.

18. Nona Lyons, Beth Stroble, and John Fischetti, "The Idea of the University in an Age of School Reform: The Shaping Force of Professional Development Schools," in Marsha Levine and Roberta Trachtman (eds.), *Making Professional Development Schools Work: Politics, Practice, and Policy* (New York: Teachers College Press, 1997), pp. 106–107.

19. Nina Bascia, "Caught in the Crossfire: Restructuring, Collaboration, and the 'Problem' School," *Urban Education* 31 (May 1996): 183.

20. Russell T. Osguthorpe and Robert S. Patterson, *Balancing the Tensions of Change* (Thousand Oaks, Calif.: Corwin, 1998), p. vii.

21. Sharon P. Robinson and Linda Darling-Hammond, "Change for Collaboration and Collaboration for Change: Transforming Teaching Through School-University Partnerships," in Linda Darling-Hammond (ed.), *Professional Development Schools: Schools for Developing a Profession* (New York: Teachers College Press, 1994), p. 207.

22. Robinson and Darling-Hammond, "Change for Collaboration," p. 206.

23. Robinson and Darling-Hammond, "Change for Collaboration," p. 217.

24. Sandholtz and Finan, "Blurring the Boundaries," pp. 17–18.

25. Coombs and Hansen, "Lessons Learned," p. 214.

26. Robinson and Darling-Hammond, "Change for Collaboration," p. 211.

27. Lyons, Stroble, and Fischetti, "Idea of the University," p. 107.

28. Lyons, Stroble, and Fischetti, "Idea of the University," p. 89.

29. Judy Peters, Rosie Dobbins, and Bruce Johnson, "Collaborative Learning Through School-University Partnerships" (paper presented at Australian Association for Research in Education Conference, Singapore, November 1996), pp. 25–29. Available at http://www.swin.edu.au/aare/conf96/DOBBR96.071. Accessed July 1998.

30. Robinson and Darling-Hammond, "Change for Collaboration," p. 212.

31. Trubowitz, "What Works," p. 214.

32. Smith, "Professional Partnerships," p. 241.

33. Lyons, Stroble, and Fischetti, "Idea of the University," p. 90.

34. Osguthorpe and Patterson, *Balancing the Tensions*, pp. 38–39.

35. Ann Lieberman, "Practices That Support Teacher Development: Transforming Conceptions of Professional Learning," *Phi Delta Kappan* 76 (April 1995): 593.

36. Solon T. Kimball and James E. McClellan Jr., *Education and the New America* (New York: Random House, 1962), p. 295.

37. Trubowitz, "What Works," p. 213.

38. Sandholtz and Finan, "Blurring the Boundaries," p. 24.

39. John I. Goodlad, *Educational Renewal: Better Teachers, Better Schools* (San Francisco: Jossey-Bass, 1994), p. 19.

40. Christenson and others, "Collaboration in Support of Change," p. 188.

41. Coombs and Hansen, "Lessons Learned," p. 216.

42. Judith Haymore Sandholtz and Katherine K. Merseth, "Collaborating Teachers in a Professional Development School: Inducements and Contributions," *Journal of Teacher Education* 43 (September–October 1992): 316.

43. Bernard R. Gifford, "The Evolution of the School-University Partnership for Educational Renewal," *Education and Urban Society* 19 (November 1986): 88.

44. Sandholtz and Merseth, "Collaborating Teachers," p. 317.

45. Brookhart and Loadman, "School-University Collaboration," p. 3.

46. Sandholtz and Merseth, "Collaborating Teachers," p. 317.

47. Cheryl L. Rosaen and Elaine Hoekwater, "Collaboration: Empowering Educators to Take Charge," *Contemporary Education* 61 (Spring 1990): 144–151.

48. Lieberman, "Practices That Support Teacher Development," p. 595.

49. Lieberman, "Practices That Support Teacher Development," p. 595.

Chapter Three

1. Some descriptions of the important participants in simultaneous renewal refer only to "faculty." This term is intended to include administrators in education, the arts and sciences, and the schools as well.

2. Quoted in John I. Goodlad, *Educational Renewal: Better Teachers, Better Schools* (San Francisco: Jossey-Bass, 1994), p. 3.

3. B. Othanel Smith, *A Design for a School of Pedagogy* (Washington, D.C.: U.S. Department of Education, 1980), pp. 6–7.

4. Goodlad, *Educational Renewal*, p. 10.

5. Some National Network for Educational Renewal settings, for lack of a comparable noun, have adopted an adjective, dubbing these three groups the *tripartite*. That term will be used throughout this book.

6. Goodlad, *Educational Renewal*, p. 1.

7. Goodlad, *Educational Renewal*, p. 23.

8. Peter Senge, *The Fifth Discipline: The Art and Practice of the Learning Organization* (New York: Doubleday, 1994), p. 206.

9. Goodlad, *Educational Renewal*, p. 19. See also John I. Goodlad and Timothy J. McMannon (eds.), *The Public Purpose of Education and Schooling* (San Francisco: Jossey-Bass, 1997).

10. Goodlad, *Educational Renewal*, pp. 19–20.

11. Goodlad, *Educational Renewal*, p. 20.

12. Goodlad, *Educational Renewal*, p. 20.

13. Ernest Boyer, *Scholarship Reconsidered: Priorities of the Professoriate* (Princeton, N.J.: Carnegie Foundation for the Advancement of Teaching, 1990); and Charles E. Glassick, Mary Taylor Huber, and Gene Maeroff, *Scholarship Assessed: Evaluation of the Professoriate* (San Francisco: Jossey-Bass, 1997).

14. John Dewey, "The Relation of Theory to Practice in Education," in Charles A. McMurry (ed.), *The Third Yearbook of the National Society for the Scientific Study of Education*, part 1, *The Relation of Theory to Practice in the Education of Teachers* (Chicago: University of Chicago Press, 1904), pp. 10–11. For a further discussion, see Roger Soder and Kenneth A. Sirotnik, "Beyond Reinventing the Past: The Politics of Teacher Education," in John I. Goodlad, Roger Soder, and Kenneth A. Sirotnik (eds.), *Places Where Teachers Are Taught* (San Francisco: Jossey-Bass, 1990), p. 404; and Goodlad, *Educational Renewal*, pp. 176–177.

15. See, for example, Hugh Petrie (ed.), *Professionalization, Partnership, and Power: Building Professional Development Schools* (Albany: State University of New York Press, 1995).

16. Trish Stoddart, "The Professional Development School: Building

Bridges Between Cultures," in Petrie (ed.), *Professionalization, Partnership, and Power*, pp. 44–45.

17. Kenneth A. Sirotnik, "Making School-University Partnerships Work," *Metropolitan Universities* 2 (Summer 1991): 19–23.

18. Michael Fullan, *Change Forces: Probing the Depths of Educational Reform* (Bristol, Pa.: Falmer, 1993).

19. Sirotnik, "Making School-University Partnerships Work," p. 20.

20. Goodlad, *Educational Renewal*, p. 74.

21. John I. Goodlad, *Teachers for Our Nation's Schools* (San Francisco: Jossey-Bass, 1990), p. 278.

22. John I. Goodlad, "Connecting the Present to the Past," in Goodlad, Soder, and Sirotnik (eds.), *Places Where Teachers Are Taught*, p. 30.

23. Goodlad, "Connecting the Present," p. 33.

24. Goodlad, *Teachers for Our Nation's Schools*, p. 278.

Chapter Four

1. "The Center of Pedagogy" (internal document, Montclair State University, Upper Montclair, N.J., January 1997), p. 2.

2. The state college-university system encompasses Montclair State University, William Paterson University, Rowan University, Kean University, Stockton State College, Jersey City State College, Ramapo State College, Edison State College, and the College of New Jersey (formerly Trenton State College), each with its own board of trustees. The other public universities in the state are Rutgers University, the University of Medicine and Dentistry of New Jersey, and the New Jersey Institute of Technology. New Jersey colleges and universities are coordinated by the Commission on Higher Education, which has some role in mission coordination and advocacy for higher education. Seven of the state colleges or universities, twelve private universities, and Rutgers offer programs in teacher education.

3. In the New Jersey Network for Educational Renewal, a partner school is one with a significant number of faculty and administrators

committed to the Agenda for Education in a Democracy and in which student teachers are placed. A professional development school has these qualities as well, along with a commitment to inquiry and the presence of university faculty on a regular basis.

4. *Montclair State Teachers College Catalog* (1928), p. 20. Much of the historical background was derived from the work of Lise Greene, Office of the President of Montclair State University, who generously shared research undertaken for her dissertation.

5. John I. Goodlad, "Connecting the Present to the Past," in John I. Goodlad, Roger Soder, and Kenneth A. Sirotnik (eds.), *Places Where Teachers Are Taught* (San Francisco: Jossey-Bass, 1990), p. 20.

6. Nicholas Michelli, one of the authors of this book, has a perhaps unique perspective on the period. He was a student at Montclair State College from 1960 to 1964, joined the faculty in 1970, and became dean of education in 1980.

7. Author's notes from interviews with faculty in the liberal arts and teacher education.

8. By the time the School of Professional Studies became the College of Education and Human Services, there had been several other reorganizations. For example, the Departments of Health Professions, Physical Education, and Recreation and Leisure Studies had been merged into one department. The Department of Industrial Studies had been dissolved, and its program to prepare technology teachers was incorporated into Curriculum and Teaching. Finally, the Department of Home Economics became the Department of Human Ecology.

9. Robert A. Pines was director of teacher education from this point until 1995.

10. For an overview of the theoretical underpinnings of the program, see Matthew Lipman, *Philosophy Goes to School* (Philadelphia: Temple University Press, 1988); and Matthew Lipman, *Thinking in Education* (Cambridge: Cambridge University Press, 1991).

11. The dean was aware of Goodlad's work. In the previous two years, the dean had served on the board of directors of the American As-

sociation of Colleges for Teacher Education when Goodlad was president-elect and president of the association. Together they had planned one of the summer leadership institutes of the association.

12. For a description of the dimensions of teaching, see John I. Goodlad, *Educational Renewal: Better Teachers, Better Schools* (San Francisco: Jossey-Bass, 1994).

13. "The Portrait of a Teacher" (Upper Montclair, N.J.: Montclair State University Center of Pedagogy, January 1997). The "Portrait" was originally developed by a committee chaired by Tina Jacobowitz, professor in MSU's Department of Reading and Educational Media and coordinator of MSU's Agenda for Education in a Democracy.

14. See Tina Jacobowitz and Nicholas M. Michelli, "Montclair State University and the New Jersey Network for Educational Renewal," in Wilma F. Smith and Gary D Fenstermacher (eds.), *Leadership for Educational Renewal: Developing a Cadre of Leaders* (San Francisco: Jossey-Bass, 1999).

15. "The New Jersey Network for Educational Renewal" (Upper Montclair, N.J.: Montclair State University Center of Pedagogy, July 1997).

16. "New Jersey Network for Educational Renewal."

17. "Center of Pedagogy," p. 2.

18. Goodlad, *Educational Renewal*, p. 10.

19. For the 1998–1999 academic year, school districts serving under twenty-five hundred students paid $2,225 in dues, and those serving over twenty-five hundred students paid $3,000. Other institutions pay dues assessed on a sliding scale.

20. Richard A. Lynde, "The Faculty Scholarship Incentive Program at Montclair State University" (paper presented at the American Association of State Colleges and Universities meeting, Lake Tahoe, July 27–30, 1997), p. 1.

21. Ernest Boyer, *Scholarship Reconsidered* (Princeton, N.J.: Carnegie Commission for the Advancement of Teaching, 1990).

22. Boyer, *Scholarship Reconsidered*, pp. 23–24.

23. Richard A. Lynde and others, "Faculty Scholarship Incentive Program: Policy and Procedures" (Upper Montclair, N.J.: Montclair State University Provost's Office, 1996), pp. 3–4.

24. Lynde and others, "Faculty Scholarship Incentive Program," p. 4.

25. College of Education and Human Services, Office of the Dean, "Academic Goals" (Upper Montclair, N.J.: Montclair State University, 1994).

26. Lynde, "Faculty Scholarship Incentive Program at MSU," p. 5.

27. Lynde, "Faculty Scholarship Incentive Program at MSU," pp. 5–6.

28. See the survey reported in Chapter Eight of this book.

29. National Commission on Teaching & America's Future, *What Matters Most: Teaching for America's Future* (New York: National Commission on Teaching & America's Future, 1996).

30. See the description of Wright State University in Chapter Eight of this book.

31. John I. Goodlad, *Teachers for Our Nation's Schools* (San Francisco: Jossey-Bass, 1990), pp. 54–64.

32. *Montclair State Teachers College Catalog*, p. 51.

Chapter Five

1. John I. Goodlad, *Teachers for Our Nation's Schools* (San Francisco: Jossey-Bass, 1990), pp. 278–306.

2. John I. Goodlad, *Educational Renewal: Better Teachers, Better Schools* (San Francisco: Jossey-Bass, 1994), p. 2.

3. Goodlad, *Educational Renewal*, p. 2.

4. John I. Goodlad, "Linking Schools and Universities: Symbiotic Partnerships," Occasional Paper no. 1 (Seattle: Center for Educational Renewal, College of Education, University of Washington, 1986, rev. 1987), pp. 19–20.

5. Goodlad, *Educational Renewal*, pp. 4–5.

6. For a detailed description of the BYU-PSP leadership associates program, see Robert S. Patterson and Kathleen H. Hughes, "The

Utah Associates Program for Leaders," in Wilma F. Smith and Gary D Fenstermacher (eds.), *Leadership for Educational Renewal: Developing a Cadre of Leaders* (San Francisco: Jossey-Bass, 1999).

7. Russell T. Osguthorpe and Robert S. Patterson, *Balancing the Tensions of Change: Eight Keys to Collaborative Educational Renewal* (Thousand Oaks, Calif.: Corwin, in press).

8. Alan A. Wilkins (BYU academic vice president) to Robert S. Patterson (BYU dean), April 14, 1998.

Chapter Six

1. Francis L. Fugate, *Frontier College: Texas Western at El Paso—The First Fifty Years* (El Paso: Texas Western, 1964), p. 8.

2. For a discussion of this tension, see Charles E. Silberman, *Crisis in the Classroom: The Remaking of American Education* (New York: Random House, 1970).

3. Fugate, *Frontier College*, p. 32.

4. Fugate, *Frontier College*, p. 48.

5. Fugate, *Frontier College*, p. 58.

6. John I. Goodlad, *Teachers for Our Nation's Schools* (San Francisco: Jossey-Bass, 1990), pp. 272–274.

7. Silberman, *Crisis in the Classroom*, p. 425.

8. Goodlad, *Teachers for Our Nation's Schools*.

9. National Commission on Excellence in Education, *A Nation at Risk: The Imperative for Educational Reform* (Washington, D.C.: U.S. Government Printing Office, 1983).

10. For a history of a century of declining public confidence in the schools, including the decline of the 1980s and 1990s, see David B. Tyack and Larry Cuban, *Tinkering Toward Utopia: A Century of Public School Reform* (Cambridge, Mass.: Harvard University Press, 1995).

11. See, for example, the recent focus on El Paso as a success story in Lynn Olson and Caroline Hendrie, "Pathways to Progress," *Education Week*, January 8, 1998, pp. 32–34.

12. Diana Natalicio, "Fall 1992 Convocation Remarks" (El Paso: University of Texas at El Paso, 1992), pp. 17–18.

13. For a discussion of the postulates and their implications, see John I. Goodlad, *Educational Renewal: Better Teachers, Better Schools* (San Francisco: Jossey-Bass, 1994), pp. 72–94.

14. For a discussion of the role of senior leadership in bringing about this change, see Arturo Pacheco, "University Commitment to Simultaneous Renewal," *Record in Educational Leadership* 15 (Spring–Summer 1995): 42–44.

Chapter Seven

1. Diana Wyllie Rigden, "What Teachers Have to Say About Teacher Education," *Perspective* 8 (Fall 1996): 1–20; and Steve Farkas and Jean Johnson, *Different Drummers: How Teachers of Teachers View Public Education* (New York: Public Agenda, 1997).

2. See the very interesting analysis of ten years of Holmes Group effort: Michael Fullan and others, *The Rise and Stall of Teacher Education Reform* (Washington, D.C.: American Association of Colleges for Teacher Education, 1998).

3. Michael G. Fullan and Matthew B. Miles, "Getting Reform Right: What Works and What Doesn't," *Phi Delta Kappan* 73 (June 1992): 746.

4. John I. Goodlad, *Educational Renewal: Better Teachers, Better Schools* (San Francisco: Jossey-Bass, 1994), pp. 10–11.

5. Fullan and others, *Rise and Stall*, 43.

Chapter Eight

1. John I. Goodlad, *Teachers for Our Nation's Schools* (San Francisco: Jossey-Bass, 1990), pp. 278–377.

2. "Forum for Educational Inquiry: A Re-creation of the Furman University Teacher Education Program" (internal document, Furman University, Greenville, S.C., 1996).

3. This description of the California Polytechnic site is based on corre-

spondence with Leonard Davidman, coordinator of the Coalition of Partner Schools.

4. "An Overview of the Hawaii School University Partnership" (internal document, University of Hawaii at Manoa, July 1997), p. 4.

5. "Overview of the Hawaii School University Partnership," p. 6.

6. "The Hawaii Institute for Educational Partnerships" (internal document, University of Hawaii at Manoa, March 27, 1998), p. 2.

7. "Hawaii Institute for Educational Partnerships," p. 3.

8. This description of the Connecticut site is based on correspondence with Dean Richard Schwab of the University of Connecticut School of Education.

9. Correspondence from Lynn K. Rhodes, associate dean of teacher education, University of Colorado at Denver.

10. John I. Goodlad, *Educational Renewal: Better Teachers, Better Schools* (San Francisco: Jossey-Bass, 1994), pp. 77–78.

11. "College-wide Plan and Procedures for Establishing the Center for Teacher Education" (internal document, College of Education, University of New Mexico, Albuquerque, Jan. 5, 1998).

12. Board of Regents of the University System of Georgia, "Board Actions to Implement the Principles for the Preparation of Educators for the Schools" (Atlanta: Board of Regents of the University System of Georgia, July 8, 1998), pp. 5–6. The evolution of the policy was shepherded by Jan Kettlewell, assistant vice chancellor of academic affairs of the Board of Regents of the University System of Georgia. Kettlewell was dean of the School of Education and Allied Professions at Miami University of Ohio, which is a member of the NNER.

13. Within the National Network for Educational Renewal, three state partnerships—Colorado's, South Carolina's, and Nebraska's—constitute individual settings.

Afterword

1. Nathalie Gehrke draws on her experience with school-university collaboration in describing the dysfunctional character of the

"trophy mentality" that seeks to advertise the product's availability before the hard work has been done (or sometimes even begun). See Nathalie J. Gehrke, "Simultaneous Improvement of Schooling and the Education of Teachers: Creating a Collaborative Consciousness," *Metropolitan Universities* 2 (Summer 1991): 43–50.

2. Howard Gardner, *Frames of Mind: The Theory of Multiple Intelligences* (New York: Basic Books, 1983), p. 70.

3. John Dewey to President William Rainey Harper of the University of Chicago, 1896(?). See John Dewey, *The Early Works, 1882–1898* (ed. Jo Ann Boydston), vol. 5, *1895–1898: Early Essays* (Carbondale: Southern Illinois University Press, 1972), p. 433.

4. B. Othanel Smith, *A Design for a School of Pedagogy* (Washington, D.C.: U.S. Department of Education, 1980).

5. Dewey to Harper.

6. Abraham Flexner, *Medical Education in the United States and Canada* (New York: Carnegie Foundation for the Advancement of Teaching, 1910).

7. John I. Goodlad, *Educational Renewal: Better Teachers, Better Schools* (San Francisco: Jossey-Bass, 1994), pp. 2–3.

8. John I. Goodlad, *Teachers for Our Nation's Schools* (San Francisco: Jossey-Bass, 1990), p. 239.

9. John I. Goodlad, *A Place Called School* (New York: McGraw-Hill, 1984).

10. Goodlad, *Teachers for Our Nation's Schools.*

11. Wilma F. Smith and Gary D Fenstermacher (eds.), *Leadership for Educational Renewal: Developing a Cadre of Leaders* (San Francisco: Jossey-Bass, 1999).

12. Alan R. Tom, *Redesigning Teacher Education* (Albany: State University of New York Press, 1997), p. 219.

13. Seymour Sarason's powerful indictment of our national political leaders in this regard is, at this time of writing, being largely ignored. See his *Political Leadership and Educational Failure* (San Francisco: Jossey-Bass, 1998).

14. Timothy J. McMannon has documented the degree to which claims of greater efficiency have influenced educational policy and practice when moral claims have failed to win the day. See his *Morality, Efficiency, and Reform: An Interpretation of the History of American Education*, Work in Progress Series no. 5 (Seattle: Institute for Educational Inquiry, 1995).

Index